# DESIGN to
# RENOURISH
## SUSTAINABLE GRAPHIC DESIGN IN PRACTICE

# DESIGN to RENOURISH

## SUSTAINABLE GRAPHIC DESIGN IN PRACTICE

ERIC BENSON
YVETTE PERULLO

CRC Press
Taylor & Francis Group
Boca Raton  London  New York

CRC Press is an imprint of the
Taylor & Francis Group, an **informa** business

A CHAPMAN & HALL BOOK

CRC Press
Taylor & Francis Group
6000 Broken Sound Parkway NW, Suite 300
Boca Raton, FL 33487-2742

© 2017 by Taylor & Francis Group, LLC
CRC Press is an imprint of Taylor & Francis Group, an Informa business

No claim to original U.S. Government works

Printed on acid-free paper
Version Date: 20160614

International Standard Book Number-13: 978-1-138-91661-6 (Paperback)

This book contains information obtained from authentic and highly regarded sources. Reasonable efforts have been made to publish reliable data and information, but the author and publisher cannot assume responsibility for the validity of all materials or the consequences of their use. The authors and publishers have attempted to trace the copyright holders of all material reproduced in this publication and apologize to copyright holders if permission to publish in this form has not been obtained. If any copyright material has not been acknowledged please write and let us know so we may rectify in any future reprint.

### Library of Congress Cataloging-in-Publication Data

Names: Benson, Eric, 1975- author. | Perullo, Yvette, author.
Title: Design to renourish : sustainable graphic design in practice / Eric Benson and Yvette Perullo.
Description: Boca Raton : Taylor & Francis, 2016. | Includes bibliographical references and index.
Identifiers: LCCN 2016018606 | ISBN 9781138916616 (alk. paper)
Subjects: LCSH: Graphic arts--Environmental aspects. | Commercial art--Environmental aspects.
Classification: LCC NC997 .B38 2016 | DDC 740--dc23
LC record available at https://lccn.loc.gov/2016018606

**Visit the Taylor & Francis Web site at**
**http://www.taylorandfrancis.com**

**and the CRC Press Web site at**
**http://www.crcpress.com**

Printed and bound in the United States of America by Sheridan

# CONTENTS

# FOREWORD

What did you want to be when you were growing up? I'm going to guess that very few people reading this will say "graphic designer." I certainly didn't. Like most people, I wanted to be a rock 'n' roll space pirate. I also wanted to make the world a better place.

Unlike many people, though, I actually grew up familiar with graphic design, since my father taught it at a local university for over 30 years. I also grew up believing I could change the world for the better, because my mother started bringing me to social justice rallies and protests before I could even walk. By the time I came around to graphic design as a career choice, I had already graduated from college and was a full-on committed activist. So my challenge was how to merge these two parts of my life.

**Graphic design is *not* the best way to change the world.** There are plenty of other ways to have a real, direct impact on people's lives. You could be volunteering in impoverished communities (here and abroad); you could start a nonprofit organization to work on social issues; you could be working to elect candidates who share your worldview; heck, you could be running for office yourself! But the fact of the matter is, if that appealed to you, you'd probably already be doing it.

I got into graphic design because I enjoyed the creative problem-solving challenges it offered and the fact that I could use my artistic skills in a way that would actually pay my bills. But I realized early on that I would need to make my chosen career and my personal ethics align if I was going to actually find any sustainable joy in life. It was at that point that I discovered the real potential for positive transformation that graphic design offered. Here was a field that was essentially touching every aspect of people's lives, every day, everywhere around the world—for better or worse.

The problem of course is the "worse" part. Graphic designers are complicit in an industry that creates literal mountains of waste, contributes to the destruction of natural habitats, and poisons waterways and the atmosphere. And that's just the tip of the socially conscious iceberg. There is a much larger web of potential impact that spirals out from the computer you work on every day—from the treatment of workers at all stages along the production process to the powerful messages about body image, happiness, gender roles, and so much more that are being conveyed in the things we design. As graphic designers, we shape the world we live in both figuratively and literally. The good news is that you can use this power to do something better.

**Doing good with graphic design is *not* easy.** When I started out in this field in the early 1990s, there was no instruction manual for being a socially conscious graphic designer. Before the Internet arrived, finding like-minded people to learn from and collaborate with was extremely difficult. There were a smattering of books that touched on the topic, but their focus was mainly on industrial design and manufacturing. It would be years before I started discovering invaluable resources online like Re-nourish (www.re-nourish.org) and the people behind it. In the meantime I had to find a way to put my idea of ethical design into practice, and it took a lot of trial and error to figure out a system that would sustain the world and myself.

For example, I was once given the opportunity to do the most sustainable letter-head design possible for a very forward-thinking client. I could work with expen-sive (at the time) tree-free paper, print on a vintage letterpress, and use inks based on vegetable oil. Of course, these inks were not readily available at the time, but I found a supplier across the country willing to send me a small container of it—enough for one print job. The box arrived at my office filled with Styrofoam pack-ing peanuts, and I realized that any net benefit I had from avoiding the petroleum in the ink was more than compensated by both the petroleum-based materials used to package it and the fuel used for shipping it across the country. It was a stark reminder of the difficulties involved in trying to do good with design and the problem with having a narrow view of what constituted doing good work. In the intervening years, I realized that a much more nuanced approach was required to make a real impact.

And that's what's marvelous about what Yvette and Eric have put together in this book. They've done the footwork, so you don't have to start from scratch. They offer practical advice and a clear systematic approach to making real change hap-pen through your daily work as a designer. True, graphic design is not the best way to change the world, but it has the potential to be a really, really good way. It's not about doing less bad, it's not about achieving a net zero impact, but it's about actually making the world a better place.

As a designer you have the opportunity to be at the forefront of a transformation for good. Are you ready to renourish our world? If so, read on...

Noah Scalin
*Founder, Another Limited Rebellion*
*Richmond, Virginia*

P.S. Doing good with design may seem to be something for just the activists, but caring about the environment is not radical and it's not a political issue. It affects us all. Everyone needs air to breathe and clean water to drink, so we're all in this together. And when you realize that you can make a difference with the work you do every day, suddenly the extra work involved becomes less of a burden.

# AUTHORS

Eric Benson was born in Arizona and raised in mid-Michigan where he later earned his BFA in graphic and industrial design from the University of Michigan, Ann Arbor, in 1998. His MFA thesis at the University of Texas, Austin, became the award-winning sustainable design website www.re-nourish.org. His work with Re-nourish translated into an academic career teaching graphic design at the University of Illinois at Urbana-Champaign. At Illinois, he runs Fresh Press Agri-Fiber Paper Lab, where he explores sustainable papermaking using corn stover, soy stalks, prairie grasses, and other waste fibers from local farms.

Eric's creative works have garnered numerous design awards and are exhibited in notable venues like the Walker Art Center, the Smithsonian Cooper Hewitt National Design Museum, the Hammer Museum, the Contemporary Arts Museum Houston, and Rhode Island School of Design (RISD).

Yvette Perullo is a Boston-based designer and educator who believes good design values people and the environment, and improves lives. She earned her MFA in visual communications design from Purdue University, West Lafayette, Indiana, and her MA degree in graphic design from the New England School of Art & Design at Suffolk University, Boston, Massachusetts where her research focused on developing tools and resources to encourage sustainable design practices—the foundation of her work with Re-nourish.

She has lectured internationally on sustainable graphic design and as a design educator, Yvette focuses on integrating sustainability methodology into her courses. Yvette is the lead designer at Bartlett Interactive in Concord, Massachusetts, an agency with a commitment to sustainability and triple bottom line business practices.

Re-nourish is an award-winning and internationally recognized nonprofit organization that provides lectures, workshops, podcasts, and online tutorials to help designers create sustainably. The website provides resources and tools like a searchable greener paper database, a print project calculator, and a green certification system for studios/creative teams and projects.

# INTRODUCTION: THIS BOOK AS A CASE STUDY

*"Designers are certainly among those whose positive contributions are essential to the building of a more humane world."*[1]

—Victor Margolin

When writing this book, we both went through the same serendipitous experience one thousand miles apart in the same week. While grocery shopping—Eric in Illinois and Yvette in Massachusetts—we noticed (more so than usual) the copious amounts of packaging and plastic that filled each fluorescently lit aisle. All of the graphic design in the grocery stores is just making a short pit stop before an eternity in the landfill. We both vividly remember feeling deflated yet more motivated than ever to inspire change as we discussed the experience after our coinciding shopping trips. Waste, and the endless connected problems associated with it, is a *wicked problem*. It seems like it can't be solved. We asked how can—and *will*—our profession ever evolve? Is it hopeless? What can we do?

Despite our good intentions at Re-nourish, we knew that behind all of the choices of paperboard boxes, plastic wrap, and styrofoam, there were designers churning out more waste, Lunchable after Lunchable and one 100-calorie pack after another. Individually wrapped and packaged to withstand a zombie apocalypse, all of these wasted resources make us wonder what we are doing to the planet, our health, and to our future economy?

It's those questions that brought us together originally as a team. Since 2008, we have been working together with the sole goal of making the outcomes of the graphic design profession sustainable. To do so, we created Re-nourish, a non-profit organization that provides online interactive tools, resources, a podcast, and consulting to create a positive change in our field.

Since being introduced at an AIGA (The Professional Association for Design) conference in Baltimore, Maryland, the two of us have continued researching, talking to, and collaborating with designers and educators, while also learning and delving deeper down the "rabbit hole." We've lectured, written articles, and advised on many design and writing projects. As we are also educators, we've integrated the topic into our classrooms (sometimes not so successfully) and into our own personal work (more successfully). Eric has even been making and researching agricultural waste paper (corn stover, tomato vines, and prairie grasses to name a few) to test its commercial viability over paper from trees at Fresh Press, the microbrewery of paper, at the University of Illinois. What we have discovered over time is that sustainable graphic design for client-based projects was not happening as often or entering the mainstream as quickly as we hoped. The book was created to help speed up things by inspiring you and providing practical know-how to not only design to avoid possible negative effects but also design to create positive outcomes using a better process called systems thinking.

"So in the spirit of sustainability, why produce a book at all?" you might wonder.

To which we reply, "Good question!"

Let us explain...

The decision to write and produce a book was not an easy one. The publishing industry does not have a stellar reputation for being environmentally friendly. We pondered the idea of expanding our website instead; however, although the Re-nourish website serves as an online toolkit and contains inspirational and useful resources and case studies for designers, there was a need to dive a bit deeper than what an online platform can offer.

There was another, more pressing reason as to why producing a physical book was important. We were up to the challenge of trying to make this book a case study— to push the boundaries of publishing. According to the Green Press Initiative, each year 30 million trees are used to make books sold in the United States alone.[2] While more and more publishers pledge to increase their use of sustainability certified paper with more recycled content, sadly it's not quite mainstream yet and it's also not enough. So we embarked on a two-year journey to make this book a case study and challenge the publishing industry to be more sustainable. Our goal was to produce a book that would be printed and bound in a manner that exemplifies the Re-nourish criteria for sustainability. As William McDonough and Michael Braungart stated in their 2002 book *Cradle to Cradle*, "this book is not a tree." Instead, it was published using "recyclable" ink and plastic paper that could be infinitely recycled after the book's useful days were over. We used *Cradle to Cradle* and their follow-up book *The Upcycle*, which is printed on chlorine-free paper with the same plastic paper cover, certified by the Forest Stewardship Council (FSC), as a baseline to make even bigger strides with our production.

After countless discussions with sustainability experts in the paper, printing, and forestry industries, we were able to put together an ideal list of requirements to make this book happen as sustainably as possible. These conversations led us to choosing Step Forward Paper™. Their commercial printing paper is made from 60% wheat straw waste and 40% tree fiber certified by FSC®. Even with their manufacturing facilities currently set up in India, Step Forward Paper has among the lowest greenhouse gas emissions and the smallest environmental impact among all papers currently available in the marketplace. In fact, in a 2014 life cycle study, their paper ended up with around 50% smaller footprint than exclusively virgin tree fiber paper.[3] Although 100% post-consumer recycled paper has a slightly better environmental rating than Step Forward Paper (possibly due to its current geographic location), paper made from agricultural residue fiber holds the potential to move away from using tree fiber altogether. This is the kind of positive market and inspirational impact we hoped to make by writing this book.

After choosing the paper, our online Re-nourish Project Calculator helped us to determine the optimum trim size of our work by "designing backward." Using a 25″ × 38″ press sheet, we determined that an 6-3/4″ × 9-1/2″ final page size printed with no bleeds was the most efficient in maximizing the press sheet. With these design decisions, the trim waste on each press sheet was reduced to a grand total of 6″ at the bottom, which we would donate to a worthy nonprofit organization for a minimally sized print job. As part of our mission, we were also determined (and in the end successful) to print the book in the United States where we are located and, as you'll learn more about in Chapter 2, use systems thinking to reduce the entire environmental footprint of this book. Furthermore, we aspired to work with a printer with a strong ecologically and socially sound mission for their business: one that held environmental and work-safe employee certifications, that stocked and promoted high-content post-consumer recycled paper, that used low-VOC (volatile organic compounds) solvents and vegetable-based inks, that offered cold-glue melt for binding, that paid living wages, and that is located regionally to other vendors related to the production of the book.

Even after a year and a half of researching for and negotiating with the publisher, we were not able to achieve all of our goals to promote this book as a case study. Much to our dismay in the end, our publisher was not as dedicated to our goals as they had originally indicated. Cost was always the deciding factor in every decision (as one would guess). When we found ways to trim waste to save a buck that we could then reinvest in better materials and processes for publishing the book, the complex system of existing contracts our publisher had with vendors restricted any real social and environmental progress. (Publishers work exclusively with select printers and are usually unlikely to source printing elsewhere.) The summer and fall of 2015 were spent haggling over printers and paper. The story is worthy of a book all to itself where, like the bards of Shakespearean times, we would recite our arduous and prolific journey to inch the publishing industry closer to stronger environmental business practices.

But, it came time to accept the fact that we would, in the end, have very little pull over final vendor choices. We may have lost a few battles in our odyssey, but we did achieve some fairly solid victories. Here is what we were able to do:

Ultimately, this book was printed by the Sheridan Group in Chelsea, Michigan. Sheridan is FSC and Rainforest Alliance certified—two of our "must haves" in selecting a reputable printer. Despite Sheridan's efforts to source materials from ethical working conditions and comply with the FSC guidelines, their public environmental policies, however, are a bit vague. Sheridan does not have Ancient Forest Friendly or Green-e certifications or any carbon neutral programs in place. These are vital for a printer in our era of global warming to minimize negative environmental impact via logging and greenhouse gas emissions.

Sheridan was able to print this book with a premium vegetable-based ink that does not contain any petroleum oil. Once the printer and ink was decided, we turned our focus toward paper. Despite our best efforts, Sheridan was not willing to print on Step Forward Paper™ as we had hoped. The issue was twofold. The printer was concerned that the paper would cause problems on press, leaving dust and particles on the blankets, and a test run would prove too costly for the publisher and too time consuming for the printer. With the cost issue rearing its ugly head yet again, our second and third 100% post-consumer waste (PCW) paper choices were also out of contention.

In the end, our publisher presented us with their "best" option of Rolland Opaque 30% PCW paper for the cover and a 10% PCW text sheet for the interior pages. We were not enthusiastic about these options, but pleased that the printing and paper vendors were within relative close proximity to each other (Michigan and Canada) to minimize transportation emissions. Rolland paper is manufactured using biogas energy in Quebec, Canada, and is FSC and EcoLogo certified with a 30% PCW content. We were not able to get much if any information about the interior paper stock. The final 6-¾″ × 9-1/2″ book size was dictated by the publisher. The press sheet size was never disclosed, so we are unable to accurately calculate our book's final environmental impact and savings. But to provide you with an approximate level of information about our environmental savings and impact, we turned to our Re-nourish Project Calculator and the Environmental Paper Network's paper calculator.

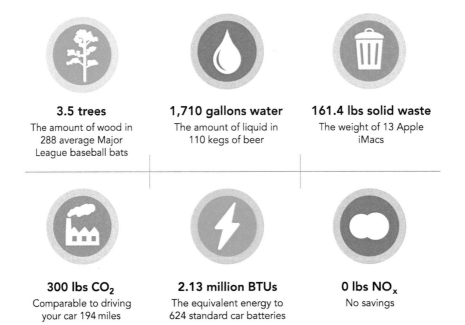

**3.5 trees**
The amount of wood in 288 average Major League baseball bats

**1,710 gallons water**
The amount of liquid in 110 kegs of beer

**161.4 lbs solid waste**
The weight of 13 Apple iMacs

**300 lbs CO₂**
Comparable to driving your car 194 miles

**2.13 million BTUs**
The equivalent energy to 624 standard car batteries

**0 lbs NO$_x$**
No savings

Figure 0.1 Approximate eco-savings for every 2000 books (about 1.355 tons of paper) on Rolland Opaque 30% PCW cover stock and a 10% PCW house stock. Calculation includes interior pages and covers.

While we hoped to make some important strides to influence market sustainability decisions with the production of this book, we feel much can be learned from our lack of success in some areas. Even in our Sisyphean efforts, we did not concede easily and negotiated back and forth with the publisher up to and past the original manuscript deadline. In the end, we believe that the more designers push that boulder uphill, the more significant strides we can and will make. Like the publishing industry, graphic design still has a long way to go. There is much progress to be made together, and that's why we wrote this book. We hope you enjoy what's next.

## ENDNOTES

1. Margolin, Victor. 2007. "Design, the Future and the Human Spirit." *Design Issues* 23 (3): 4–15.
2. "Book Sector." *Green Press Initiative*. http://www.greenpressinitiative.org/about/bookSector.htm. Accessed February 6, 2016.
3. "Expanded Comparative Life Cycle Study of Wheat Straw Paper." Step Forward Paper. September 2014. http://stepforwardpaper.com/wp-content/uploads/2013/01/Website-FINAL-PDF-Version-1.pdf. Accessed February 6, 2016.

# Chapter 1

# BEYOND THE BOTTOM LINE

"I can't imagine doing anything else." We all have most likely made this statement about the profession. Graphic design is creative and logical, expressive and practical, and demanding and fun. You wear many hats and change them frequently. You might be brainstorming logo ideas one minute and sending out invoices or estimating project plans the next. In the same day you could be delegating tasks to colleagues, providing feedback to contractors, and presenting ideas to clients. Despite the diversity of the job and the many hats you don throughout the day, most graphic designers specialize or have a distinct passion for one area of design or type of working environment. Your area of expertise may be in print, exhibition, packaging design, interactive design, or traditional advertising. You may be working in-house for a company, running your own freelance business, or working at a large agency or a small design studio. Whatever your niche, the work has a significant positive or negative impact on our world. As designers, we relish the praise of satisfied clients, recognition by peers, and the return on investment of a successful campaign, but beyond the immediate influence of the work, there is much more that may not be measured or seen. What are the unintended consequences of design work over time? How does the work impact the planet we live on? The last question is one more designers are thinking about as the realities of global warming and changes in our natural landscape like pollution, droughts, and deforestation reveal. There must be a shift in mindset away from only making beautiful and economically driven work to include a better understanding and a strategy to stop the negative impacts of design work on the planet.

In recent years, we have all witnessed too many environmental disasters like the horrific 2010 BP oil spill in the Gulf of Mexico, the 2014 tragic flooding in Pakistan, and the ongoing severe droughts and wildfires in the Western United States and Australia. It is highly likely that the latter of the series of tragedies have been fueled by global warming, one of the many reasons why design must change. Reversing global warming is the most important battle humanity faces in its history as it will have an impact on everything. It is true that the planet has experienced a warming before (roughly 6,000 years ago)[1]; however, this warming was caused by a natural cycle from cold to hot that occurs roughly every 100,000 years.[2] Starting with the industrial revolution, humanity found a way to unintentionally "hack" the climate cycle (tens of thousands of years too early). Increased greenhouse gas emissions from transportation and mass production fueled by rising consumption (where design plays a major role) is how people have changed our atmosphere. The good news is that if civilization now knows how to break a climate cycle, it also means we now know how to fix it.

But it's not just the environment and human health that will be hurt by global warming; the economy will take a major hit as well. In 2015, the magazine

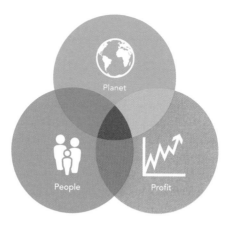

Figure 1.1 The triple bottom line.

*The Economist* commissioned a study that showed inaction on global warming would cause a loss of up to 4.2 trillion dollars[3] in the US economy alone. Designers' livelihood will clearly be negatively affected by an economic loss of this magnitude. The worldwide economy and all living things on the planet are connected, and global warming is helping us all realize this more quickly and vividly. (We will explore this interconnectedness in Chapter 2.)

Three components that global warming will affect are the environment (animals and natural resources), the economy, and the people who live in and participate in both. This is commonly referred to as the *triple bottom line* (Figure 1.1). You may have heard this term before as it refers to the pursuit of growth balanced with social, ecological, and economic needs (or people, planet, and profit). All three parts of this concept are related, linked, and integral to a truly sustainable model of living in a healthy world. When applied to graphic design, the triple bottom line helps designers understand how print and digital work impact the overall health of the world. This book is about those impacts (both positive and negative), where the profession stands today, and most importantly what we can all do to make more sustainable work.

## THE GOOD

*"The most important thing in design, it seems to me, is the consequence of your action, and whether you're interested, fundamentally, in persuading people to do things that are in their interests"*

—Milton Glaser.[4]

Graphic designers have had a hand in advancing the world economically and in shaping society and popular culture. Outcomes of design continue to help educate the public about important social issues, create tools to allow for an open exchange of information, improve the financial growth of organizations and the people that work for them, and inspire people to make a difference in peoples' lives. Graphic design work, although many times misunderstood or undervalued (if you have been asked to "make it pretty" you can relate), is an important fixture in our economy and society. If designers stopped doing their jobs, it would be very difficult for companies to communicate to their customers effectively and achieve their business or organizational missions. Beyond the questionable aesthetics that would exist without your thoughtful skills, more importantly society would face a challenge as access to valuable information would be hard to find, convoluted, and possibly even illegible. Let's face it, good design is important. It lends credibility and visibility to an organization, an idea, or a message. Not only does it make economic and cultural sense but it can also be important for the health of our environment, which we will discuss later.

Let's take a look at how effective design can have a positive economic influence. In a joint study conducted through Stanford University, it was found that a website's aesthetic qualities are the most important when people make credibility judgments about an organization online. In addition, a company is perceived as more trustworthy if their website is easy to navigate.[5] The visual design indeed directly reflects the professionalism and quality of an organization. The same perceptions learned from the web design study can then be applied to other designed material. Gaining trust from customers is paramount for a company. If a business looks legitimate and trustworthy, a potential client is more likely to do business with the organization. This begins to build a client relationship which could potentially bring return business. And since it costs five times more money to attract a new customer than it does to keep an existing one, loyal clients can help maintain a consistent revenue stream.[6] These relationships are beneficial for positive online reviews and referrals to friends and family, potentially leading to increased profits. It makes sense and cents. Good design can increase a business' bottom line through strengthened confidence in an organization's products and services. This is just one example of how graphic design continues to have a profound impact on our economy, where it can be argued, improves the standard of living for all concerned.

The results of effective graphic design also contribute significantly to making people's lives easier. As trained visual communicators, designers can turn complex information into easily digestible messages. In high-stress situations, clear signage is particularly crucial in places like airports. Many airline travelers today are tired, rushed, or anxious (or maybe all of the above!). The stress of waiting in long lines and having tight connections are compounded in a poorly laid out airport. Well-designed signage that is understandable, even for those with visual impairments, helps ease stress and anxiety so that passengers can quickly navigate to where they need to go on time. Color decisions and legible typography on screens and signage can make the difference between missing and making a flight.

Even on a small scale, thoughtful design solutions can make everyday tasks easier and a lot less frustrating. While some of us swear never to do it again, most of us have put together our fair share of ready-to-assemble furniture. And if you're like so many others, you just scan the pictures without actually reading the instructions. This is when well-done information design for a DIY bookcase instructions can make the difference between one that steadily holds your vast library of literature (preferably this book included) or one that collapses into a mangled pile of particle board and endless stream of expletives.

Making people's lives easier as graphic designers covers a wide range of areas from creating easy-to-follow assembly instructions to, more critically, signage. Visual design skills are also often put to use for worthy campaigns or causes. Human rights abuses, social inequality, environmental destruction, and even political campaigns are areas in which graphic designers have been instrumental in raising awareness and inspiring action. We discussed a bit earlier about how quality design can help build trust, and this is particularly true when motivating people to fund a worthy cause. Even the most generous of people will be wary about donating money if the organization appears less than honest. But when done well, designers' skills are helpful when shedding light on issues or motivating people to take action to help others.

Graphic designers have developed strategic branding campaigns and created innovative ideas to help worthy causes from local nonprofits to international organizations succeed. Some have motivated America's young adults to get out and vote, spread awareness and helped raise money for cancer and AIDS research, educated people about the dangers of smoking and gained support to stop offshore drilling. Graphic design has the potential to make a huge difference and greatly benefit the economy and people's day-to-day lives.

## THE BAD

### Planet

As we write this book, the levels of carbon dioxide in the atmosphere hover around 400 parts per million (ppm) according to the Mauna Loa Observatory in Hawaii. This is dangerously high. To put that number in perspective, scientists say the carbon dioxide levels must be reduced to about 350 ppm to maintain a livable and thriving planet.[7] While we can't solve this alone, designers can make more responsible decisions in the choice of project outcomes, materials, and vendors to work with. We have begun this process as a profession to "do less bad" by investing in post-consumer waste papers, vegetable-based inks, environmentally certified products, and choosing vendors powered by renewable energy. Less bad is a start but it's not enough to reverse the current trajectory. If designers only strive for their work to have a net zero impact on the planet, that would keep the levels at or around the current 400 ppm. Designers can do better. There is an opportunity to renourish our world, to create work that helps to not only educate clients and audiences but also to have a positive impact on lives and the planet while reducing the levels of carbon dioxide.

This is the 21st century design problem. Before we go into how to achieve this, let's first review some of the reasons we have come to this fork in the road.

Stylish design solutions that are created for clients usually only help create larger, unintended problems for the environment. Pulitzer prize winning author Russell Baker said, "(t)he American dream is to turn goods into trash as fast as possible."[8] And not many designed items hit the garbage bin faster than packaging—a direct-to-trash or "cradle to grave" contribution to the landfill problems. The lifespan of most packaging is incredibly short. All too often, the packaging of a product is either unnecessary or excessive and includes toxic materials like adhesives, coatings, inks, or plastics. The problems that arise in the landfills from packaging and other printed "solutions" pose an environmental and health hazard. Leachate is an example of this. Leachate is the rainwater and other liquids that filter down through the landfill encountering plastics, papers, and other materials on its way to the bottom. It contains fairly high concentrations of harmful substances from the materials it came into contact with and poses very significant environmental and human health problems as a result. A large percentage of landfills leak this hazardous leachate contaminating ground and surface water nearby.

In addition, the decomposition of garbage in landfills releases methane, a potent odorless greenhouse gas that, with carbon dioxide, are some of the largest contributors to global warming. Packaging, for instance, has significantly contributed to overflowing landfills. Ultimately, all that packaging designers put their hearts and souls into ends up as beautifully designed trash. In landfills in both United States and France, for instance, packaging that could have been recycled or avoided entirely account for anywhere between 30% and 37% of the trash.[9] This is a perfect example of why a one-way system of treasure to trash is damaging to our world and unsustainable at its core (Figure 1.2).

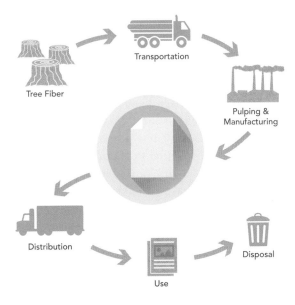

Figure 1.2 A linear paperboard supply chain.

But there is more to consider here than just the project's likely last stop—the landfill. At the beginning of a new project, for instance, the simple act of choosing paper and a printer has led to (over time) irreversible environmental damage like global warming, deforestation, and the shrinking polar ice caps. Physical projects require transportation by truck, rail, or air and are also hosted on large servers. The oil that fuels almost all the transportation and manufacturing is not only environmentally catastrophic in its drilling (recall the 2010 Gulf oil spill) but also in its own transport (for instance, the 2015 West Virginia train derailment), and in its consumption (carbon dioxide and particulate emissions that cause global warming and respiratory problems). Added to this equation are other natural resources needed for manufacturing like plastics (made from oil), metals, wood, and water.

Let's go deeper into how graphic design work needs and affects our water supply. Everything that is created, and the technology that's required, demands enormous amounts of water. The benchmark for water use in North America is 17,000 gallons per ton of paper. Multiply that by the millions of metric tons of paper produced globally and the amount of water consumed by the paper industry is hard to imagine. The computers used to create powerful and meaningful work guzzle up an enormous amount of water in their own manufacture. A single desktop computer requires an estimated 1.5 tons of water to fabricate![10] As water comes into the manufacturers to build our creations, it also flows out, but not in the same condition it entered. The polluted water enters rivers, lakes, and streams affecting clean drinking water, infecting the fish that we eat, and harming other wildlife that is dependent on this water for survival. (We'll further go into how design affects ecosystems in Chapter 2.)

## People

We are all aware to some degree how a choice of paper could negatively affect the environment, and can guess, then, that such environmental impacts may have adverse effects on human health. But much less is mentioned about that paper's effect on people and cultures. Paper companies worldwide provide quality jobs but have also been known to log forests or establish tree plantations without the consent of local communities or indigenous peoples who have rights to that land. These people rely on the local forests for food, shelter, commerce, and spiritual ties. Unfortunately, entire villages in countries like Indonesia, Brazil, and Tanzania have been forced from their land, often through the use of armed police or the military, only to have their home destroyed by logging.[11] Such practices leave the people with no means of survival. In some cases, protests against this "blood timber" have resulted in violence and casualties. Sadly, in 2014, four leaders from Peru's Ashaninka people were assassinated for opposing illegal logging on their land.[12] With so many other methods of creating quality paper from recycled or alternative fibers, why are designers still asking for and supporting the use of virgin tree fiber from old growth forests and risking such atrocities?

It's important to pose these types of questions more often and work to solve them with clients, managers, or printers.

True sustainability takes into account human health, not merely physical well-being but also strong social infrastructure, engagement, and social ties that lead to happiness and contentment. The preservation and perpetuation of strong societies and cultures are integral to the balance of the triple bottom line because for many, culture is a value system, something that is rooted in tradition, is cared about, nostalgic, or a way of life. Culture and social relationships offer happiness and comfort for many. Graphic designers have a huge influence on social and cultural sustainability through the sourcing of materials chosen for projects and the messages communicated in their work.

Designers are trained to create beautiful, persuasive work that either elicits desire in the viewer or motivates an action. Effective visual communication can convince someone to purchase a new product or change his or her political or social belief structures. Graphic designers, with the help of marketing, often contribute to campaigns that appeal to very specific "target markets." Knowing the audience or choosing a single group to focus on is imperative in order to create effective campaigns with positive returns for the clients. Unfortunately, this methodology has also been used in unethical ways to manipulate and prey on vulnerabilities. A sad example of this are the stereotyped images, language, and campaigns cigarette companies used to advertise to predominantly poor African American communities. As a result, African American smokers are the only ethnic group to have suffered disproportionately from smoking-related diseases in recent years.[13]

Another example of unethical practices in advertising includes digitally altered models and actors in fashion magazines and campaigns targeting women and teens. Designers and photographers, armed with photo imaging software, slim down already thin models, increase muscle mass, enhance breasts, and remove pimples to perpetuate the idea that "perfect" is normal—that if we don't look a certain way, we need to be "fixed." Then these ideal images are used to sell the promise of happiness and unrealistic lifestyles. A disturbing example of this involves the advertising of dietary products to teenage girls. Many young women are already self-conscious about their changing bodies and many companies have taken advantage of this. Similar advertisements for clothing, skin care, perfume, and other beauty products have used this same approach asking us to purchase more products to feel better about ourselves. With so much advertising exposure, these messages are really difficult to ignore and have a negative influence on all of our self-esteem. From an early age, we are bombarded with images and messages that reinforce the idea that to be happy and successful we must be ultrathin and flawless, which in addition to self-esteem problems can cause depression and eating disorders.[14] In fact, 65% of women and girls suffer from eating disorders. Why would we, as a profession, want to help perpetuate that dysfunction?

## Profit

However shameful it can sometimes be, advertising does work. More than $500 billion was spent on advertising globally in 2012[15] and is expected to increase by another 5.8% by the time you're reading this book.[16] Advertising lures consumers to purchase new products, too often contributing to the linear and unsustainable path of production, consumption, and disposal. Designer and educator, Victor Papanek referred to this consumerist model of "persuading people to buy things they don't need, with money they don't have, in order to impress others who don't care."[17] A one-way system of consumption and disposal results in dwindling and degraded resources. The effects of supply and demand are apparent when resources become scarce or more difficult to obtain resulting in increasing costs. This reminds us of our previous discussion on the environmental unsustainability of packaging. But outside of the environmental costs of packaging, what are the economic ones?

To start, packaging usually makes up around 10% to 20% of the cost of the items purchased.[18] It is estimated that the packaging cost of some cosmetic products and toiletries may be as high as 30% of a product's selling price.[19] This cost is one aspect that adds to both the company's and customer's budget. Finding a way to minimize the packaging size and weight will definitely have an impact on lowering cost and consequently a positive impact on the environment. The next step would be to design packaging that actually "gives back" to the planet, one that enriches the soil when composted or removes greenhouse gases from the air while keeping costs down.

Graphic design work that is expensive to produce due to costly materials, exotic finishes, or specialty processes must be compensated for elsewhere. To recoup the price associated with design and advertising, organizations or businesses may make up the amount spent in other ways. Generally, the cost is regained at the expense of the consumer or, even worse, at the expense of the worker. Consumers may be compensating for the added cost of the packaging in which case the product becomes unattainable to some people. Such a system seems acceptable when thinking about luxury items like big screen televisions, or celebrity-endorsed perfumes or watches; however, inequality becomes truly apparent when financial disparity affects basic needs items like food, medicine, education, and water. When access to these is limited due to cost, economic inequality has a negative affect across the entire triple bottom line.

As we explained using packaging as an example, many issues in each component of the triple bottom line overlap. The interconnectedness of all parts makes it impossible to divide each portion of the triple bottom line into three neat containers. It is useless to discuss packaging in isolation as an economic concern without mentioning its menace to people and the environment. As packaging impacts one component of the triple bottom line, it also affects all three.

## THE BETTER

Designers are making positive strides to forge a path toward sustainability, but there are still many obstacles to designing with the triple bottom line in mind. Faced with tight deadlines, a shortage of resources, and often a lack of support or buy-in from our manager or client, there are many challenges designers face on the job that the upcoming case studies will help answer. For instance, what can you do when proposing sustainable alternatives, but the client won't budge? Let's look at things from their perspective for a moment to understand how they see a design problem. Not being familiar with the design process and the time required for quality work, many clients wait until the last minute—they needed a design solution and they needed it yesterday. Discussing different ideas like the triple bottom line, or using a tree-free paper, or a renewable energy hosting service takes time and a willingness to listen. Add to this the time it takes to discuss the positives of more sustainable choices with the printer and you've added hours, if not days, to the project.

Clients may be more concerned with aesthetics or revenue over environmental or social impacts or possibly they have the preconceived notion that sustainable materials and vendors will be more costly than traditional ones. Some clients have such a tight budget that spending additional time on research into more responsible materials would net an hourly rate so low you might as well be working pro-bono. We do not necessarily believe that our clients intentionally want to pollute the planet, but rather time and money take precedence. That is what affects them directly and immediately. When time is short and money is tight, it's difficult for clients or project managers to look beyond the financial issues to address other larger ones. They are only focusing on the profit component of the triple bottom line.

What if a client is open to working in a more sustainable way but the deadline is tight giving you or your team little time to research or talk with vendors? Such time constraints and inadequate resources are limiting and make obtaining the knowledge needed to make responsible decisions difficult. All designers understand the need for immediacy and fast turn-around time. The short deadlines you are likely familiar with do not allow ample time for investigation into topics like sustainability that require more substantial research. There is no time! How can a design team possibly get clients to pay attention to how many trees are required to make the paper for a project or to the amount of carbon emissions from shipping the finished project from a printer in Asia when the project needs to be at the printer in an hour? Designing quickly is usually, and unfortunately, the solution. Designers need to keep clients and managers happy to keep the lights on and put healthy food on the table, so often you must do what they ask.

If you are a print designer, you may have run into the following problem one too many times. You have chosen a beautiful 100% post-consumer waste recycled paper with all of the best environmental certifications; it's Forest Stewardship Council (FSC) and Ancient Forest Friendly certified, processed chlorine-free, manufactured with renewable energy, and made locally. This paper has the perfect color and texture. But later you learn that the client only needs to print a small number of pieces, maybe just a few hundred, but paper manufacturers only sell paper in full cartons. (Purchasing a full carton when only a small quantity is needed is too expensive and wasteful.) Suddenly, the only choice is house paper that the printer has in stock.

Perhaps, you or your team has been hired to design and develop a website. After accepting the job you realize the client has already secured web hosting and registration. The hosting service is powered by conventional energy, promotes its services through sexist advertising, and has been known to have some other unethical business practices. While unsustainable, this vendor's business model does not align with the client's ethos—or yours. The design team was planning instead to run this website on an employee-owned web hosting provider powered entirely by solar and wind energy. The choice of renewable energy by the team here is important as data have a large carbon footprint. Greenpeace estimates that all the server farms and networks worldwide would rank sixth among all countries for energy use.[20] To add to this problem, the Internet is adding 830 million tons of carbon dioxide to the atmosphere annually.[21] So choosing servers powered by renewable energy is paramount. However, a better hosting service is just one way to minimize the carbon footprint when designing for web and mobile. Decreasing the download time is another smart strategy. Designers can do this by better optimizing images, videos, code, and content. In this example, less *is* more.

Design solutions that create more problems than they solve are not successful or effective graphic design. But asking how the design solution affects human health and well-being, the environment, and economic growth and equality is the first step in successful sustainable work. If designers begin by trying to improve the triple bottom line through a systems thinking approach (which we will define in Chapter 2), mapping out projects will help to visualize where certain choices have positive and negative impacts. Then designers can begin to work on creative solutions to transform all of the negative impacts into a net positive—to renourish.

This book features case studies describing how professional graphic designers developed innovative solutions to address similar scenarios described earlier. We'll look at a variety of industries, not just the sustainable ones already on board. But first, in Chapter 2, we will explain the strategy of systems thinking and how including this in the design process will create outcomes that improve the triple bottom line.

## ENDNOTES

1. "The Mid-Holocene 'Warm Period'" *NOAA*. August 20, 2008. http://www.ncdc.noaa.gov/paleo/globalwarming/holocene.html. Accessed July 23, 2015.

2. "Astronomical Theory of Climate Change." *NOAA*. April 6, 2009. Web. July 27, 2015. http://www.ncdc.noaa.gov/paleo/milankovitch.html. Accessed July 23, 2015.

3. "The Cost of Inaction: Recognizing the Value at Risk from Climate Change." *The Economist*. July 24, 2015. Web. July 27, 2015. https://www.eiuperspectives.economist.com/sites/default/files/The%20cost%20of%20inaction_0.pdf. Accessed on July 27, 2015.

4. "Milton Glaser on Making Design History." *Creative Blog*. November 25, 2009. http://www.creativebloq.com/milton-glaser-making-design-history-11094202. Accessed February 20, 2015.

5. Fogg, BJ, Leslie Marable, Julianne Stanford, and Ellen Tauber. "How Do People Evaluate a Web Site's Credibility?" *Risingline*. October 29, 2002. https://risingline.com/pdf/stanford-web-credibility.pdf. Accessed February 18, 2015.

6. Lawrence, Alex. "Five Customer Retention Tips for Entrepreneurs." *Forbes*. November 1, 2012. http://www.forbes.com/sites/alexlawrence/2012/11/01/five-customer-retention-tips-for-entrepreneurs/#11bb158417b0. Accessed February 17, 2015.

7. "$CO_2$ Now." https://www.co2.earth. Accessed February 26, 2015.

8. *Trashed*. Directed by Bill Kirkos. USA: OXI Productions, 2007. Film. http://www.trashedmovie.com.

9. "Municipal Solid Waste Generation, Recycling, and Disposal in the United States: Facts and Figures for 2012." *US Environmental Protection Agency*. February 1, 2014. https://www.epa.gov/sites/production/files/2015-09/documents/2012_msw_fs.pdf. Accessed February 18, 2015.

10. "Your Computer's Lifetime Journey." *National Resource Defense Council*. November 30, 2011. Accessed February 17, 2015.

11. The Green Press Initiative. n.d. "Impacts on People." *The Green Press Initiative*. http://www.greenpressinitiative.org/impacts/peopleImpacts.htm

12. Baquero, Carlos. "Peru and COP 20: Among Violence and Forests." *Global Rights Blog*. November 3, 2014. https://dejusticiablog.com/2014/11/03/peru-and-cop-20-among-violence-and-forests/. Accessed February 17, 2015.

13. U.S. Department of Health and Human Services. 1998. "Tobacco Use Among US Racial/Ethnic Minority Groups—African Americans, American Indians and Alaska Natives, Asian Americans and Pacific Islanders Hispanics: A Report of the Surgeon General." Atlanta, Georgia: US: Department of Health and Human Services, Centers for Disease Control and Prevention, National Center for Chronic Disease Prevention and Health Promotion, Office on Smoking and Health. https://www.cdc.gov/tobacco/data_statistics/sgr/1998/complete_report/pdfs/complete_report.pdf. Accessed February 17, 2015.

14. *Miss Representation*. Directed by Jennifer Siebel Newsom and Kimberlee Acquaro. By Atlas, J., Congdon, J., Dietrich, C., Raskin, J., and Siebel Newsom, J. USA: Virgil Films & Entertainment, Netflix, OWN: The Oprah Winfrey Network, Roco Films, 2014. Film.

15. Johnson, Bradley. "10 Things You Should Know About the Global Ad Market." *Ad Age*. December 8, 2013. http://adage.com/article/global-news/10-things-global-ad-market/245572/. Accessed February 17, 2015.

16. "Global Ad Spend Grows 3.2% in 2012." *Nielsen*. April 11, 2013. http://www. nielsen.com/us/en/insights/news/2013/global-ad-spend-grows-3.2-percent-in-2012.html.

17. Papanek, Victor J. 1985. *Design for the Real World: Human Ecology and Social Change*. 2nd ed., completely rev. Chicago, IL: Academy Chicago.

18. Lane, Christian. www.In.gredients.com. Oct 8, 2010. Web. Oct 10, 2011.

19. McDonough, William, and Michael Braungart. *The Upcycle: Beyond Sustainability—Designing for Abundance*. New York: North Point Press, 2013. 170.

20. Cook, G., Dowdall, T., Pomerantz, D., and Wang, Y. April 1, 2014. Clicking Clean: How Companies are Creating the Green Internet. http://www. greenpeace.org/usa/wp-content/uploads/legacy/Global/usa/planet3/PDFs/clickingclean.pdf. Accessed August 6, 2015.

21 American Chemical Society. "Toward reducing the greenhouse gas emissions of the Internet and telecommunications." *ScienceDaily*. www. sciencedaily.com/releases/2013/01/130102140452.htm. Accessed August 6, 2015.

# Chapter 2
# THE HAWK, THE SQUIRREL, AND THE OAK TREE

## WHAT IS SYSTEMS THINKING?

For a moment, try to remember your first semester in college. (It wasn't *that* long ago, was it?) Think about the foundational art and design courses you took that term and the vocabulary your instructor covered in the first few weeks to help you better understand the worlds of art and design. Most likely you were introduced to the German word *Gestalt* meaning "the whole is more than the sum of its parts" or a "unified whole." Understanding the concept of *Gestalt* is a good starting point to explore how to think in systems. When we discuss "systems" in this book, we are not necessarily referring to what you may have already understood as systems like letterforms in an alphabet or the components of a branding campaign, but rather to the scientific methodology used in natural sciences like biology and ecology. Environmental pioneer John Muir describes this concept most clearly: "When we try to pick out anything by itself we find that it is bound fast by a thousand invisible cords that cannot be broken, to everything in the universe."[1] In other words, everything is connected on our planet and our natural systems depend on balance. So to think in systems, when it comes to our profession, it means we approach a design problem by being informed, aware of, and influenced by the impacts that our material and vendor choices have on one another, the planet, and consequently on ourselves.

The concept of systems thinking isn't a new idea, but it is an emerging concept in the field of graphic design. For the unfamiliar, the description of systems thinking might seem unusual at first read and that is understandable since most of us have been trained to concentrate our attention on two things—how the design piece affects its intended audience and how it impacts the client's revenues. To think in systems also includes those two aspects of the project, but additionally it considers: how the work we do is demanding our natural resources?, Where and how do we get materials to produce our projects?, Who and what is affected by our decisions?, and What will happen to the project after it's handed over? It sounds a bit dizzying, but fret not, we'll describe some practical ways to work in this method a bit later in the chapter. One thing is for sure, this paradigm shift in your design process will require a time investment and some more careful and thoughtful planning and discussion with your team, vendors, and clients. However, the results of working this way will be greatly rewarding and will improve the work we do and the world we live in.

That is a pretty grand statement. Let's investigate a small example to better explain how thinking in systems can improve the work we do. Historically, a graphic design problem is addressed in isolation that usually just considers the audience and the outcome. In common design situations, the designer or design team is tasked with a pre-determined solution from a client like "design a direct mail piece to encourage voting." Typically, designers would then tackle the assignment by looking at a very small set of variables: text and image, paper, and a printer. The final format, already decided by the client, may have been chosen without first looking at the entire system of issues that cause the low voter turn-out to begin with. With a systems thinking approach, defined by MIT scientist Donella Meadows, the designer and client would visually map out the design problem including the elements (people and resources), interconnections (relationships), and intended purpose (goal) and not solely focus on the tangible designed outcome. One would need to expand their view past the printer, paper, or mobile app to understand audience relationships, boundaries, values and then to natural resources, materials, vendors, distribution, and impacts. Solving the problem would require asking questions like: "What motivates citizens to vote?", "Who are the current active voters?", "How does socioeconomics impact the political system?", and "Who do we need to collaborate with to gain better insight?" It might become clear after asking these questions and visualizing that system of interactions, that printing thousands of direct mail pieces is not the ideal solution for your client for various reasons. It is expensive, time-consuming, and damaging to the environment as a considerable amount of carbon is emitted into the atmosphere, and it may not even serve the target audience.

It's worth noting in this example that at 3%–4% response rate,[2] direct mail is often not the most effective solution to most design problems. Understanding all the project variables, purposes, and impacts can lead to more effective, targeted and responsible design. After asking meaningful questions and collaborating with the right people, the solution to the voter turnout problem may instead involve advocating change to public policies, connecting with an initiative that a nonprofit organization has already started in the community, and quite possibly developing an awareness campaign that includes alternative solutions such as digitally led creative or social media marketing.

The above example may better explain how systems thinking can benefit your design process and be a catalyst to improving the triple bottom line, but as visual people, what does it look like? One way to better visualize how thinking in systems works would be to imagine a natural food chain from the world of ecology. As children, we learned that there are predators and prey where, typically, the larger, stronger animal will eat the smaller, weaker one. For instance, a rattlesnake is nourishment for a red tailed hawk, which in turn would have preyed on a gray squirrel that relied on the acorns that dropped from a nearby oak tree. The oak tree maintains its own health from the fallen leaves, insects, and mushrooms that decompose into the soil around the roots to provide nutrients. These plants and animals are affected not only by each other but also by the climate, weather,

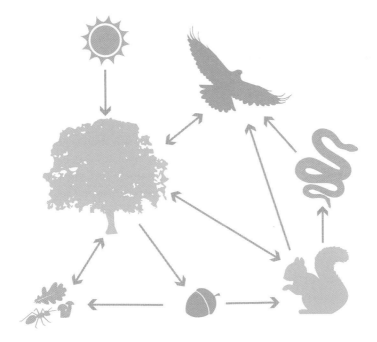

Figure 2.1 A sample biological system.

humans, or other animals. They are all interconnected, interdependent, and sustainable without negative human interventions like deforestation, urban sprawl, or pollution. They also comprise two important facets of a living system—waste equals food (or natural materials that continuously help another part of the system) and a living cycle (a circular process that repeats). In fact, a food chain, like the one mentioned above, is part of a larger food web which is just one small section of a much larger network that makes up an ecosystem. The world is definitely complex. From cells to insects, from animals to plants, from humans to machines, and everything in between are connected. When the same food chain analogy is applied to graphic design, the potential and real impacts that certain decisions have on the world around us become clear. For instance, a more responsible choice in something as seemingly simple as a paper selection could prevent unneeded carbon emissions, keep jobs in a community, and even save cute furry animals (Figure 2.1).

## GRAPHIC DESIGN IS MORE THAN THE SUM OF ITS PARTS

The graphic design profession is in itself an ecosystem. Obviously, designers rely on clients to provide paying projects, while clients depend on a graphic designer's creative and strategic expertise to resolve their communication and business needs. Besides that first level of interaction, there are many other collaborators whom you may rely on to help produce and deliver your projects and who in turn rely on you to continue to send them work. These partners include photographers, illustrators, writers, consultants, printers, paper manufacturers, developers, hosting providers, and so on—all those connected to the profession of graphic design and involved at various degrees. It doesn't stop there.

At the beginning of this chapter, we asked you to think back to your first design foundation class and recall the term *Gestalt*. Again, we'll use your design education as a means to better understand how systems affect us as graphic designers and also how it affects the world around us. In school, it's very likely you learned about two prolific designers, Charles and Ray Eames. This couple creatively and successfully dabbled in everything from graphics, furniture, sound, to film. In 1977, they released a second version of their film *Powers of Ten*, which we'll use here as an example to go deeper into the interconnected systems of the graphic design profession. *Powers of Ten* broke down the audience's understanding of the universe into factors of ten through zooming in and out of our bodies, world, and universe. The movie began with an overhead view of a relaxing picnic in a park and zoomed out and upward by a factor of ten to show the incredible size and scope of our universe. The film then zoomed back to the picnic and into the human body to microscopic scale.

Let's apply the powers of ten on the paper supply chain from the forest to the consumer as a means to show the complexity of the systems that design affects and that affect us. The paper used in design projects today predominantly comes from trees. The forest then is the starting point of the "paper trail" which becomes the magazines, books, and other print material that is created. When looking at the forest from a surface level, it can be seen solely as an input (wood) into the economy within the system. This economic input is based on the concepts of both stock and flows. They are two very important ideas to understand systems in general. In this logging scenario, the trees are called a "stock" or the resource that you can count and measure, while its movement in or out of the system (forest) is called the "flow." To keep this system sustainable (or a living cycle), one would have to ensure that the input flow of new trees (combined with overall individual tree growth) is equal to the output flow of trees being cut down (wood) or leaving the "stock." Currently, in the logging industry (and many other industries that graphic design relies upon), this system is not sustainable and is in fact broken. With a regrowth rate of thirty to a hundred years, the input flow (new trees) is not fast enough to match the current demands of the output flow (logging), which effectively means the demand exceeds the supply. In addition, as trees increase in age and size, the more carbon they continue to sequester. A newly planted tree, no matter how fast it may grow, would not, in the near future, catch up with the carbon sequestering capabilities of a more mature tree. The stock and flow of logging in our current system are unsustainable (Figure 2.2).

Zooming into this flow you can see that equipment is required to cut down a tree, and the machinery to be manufactured requires natural resources (e.g., metal). All of that metal needs to be mined or purchased from recyclers, then shipped,

**Flow**

**Inflow:** Tree growth          **Outflow:** Logging

**Stock:** Forest

Figure 2.2 Basic stock and flow of a forest.

processed, shipped again, manufactured, and shipped once more to a store or warehouse. All of these steps require energy, resources, money, and people. Unfortunately, as it currently stands, most energy production requires fossil fuels, which are in limited supply and difficult to acquire. Because this planet is of a specific measurable size, the resources available can be quantified as well. In other words, there is a limit to what is available and, in the current way of working, people are using more than the planet will be able to provide. As many of us have learned from managing a monthly budget, if we spend significantly more than what we earn, the likelihood of going into debt is quite high, and it will take months to years of cutting back to replenish the accounts. The same holds true for the planet's natural resources and the economy they provide for. Society can't grow economically forever while voraciously subtracting resources from the assets side of the balance sheet. This again is the basics of a systems stock and flow where the goal instead should be creating a living or circular cycle of consumption and regrowth (or renourish). According to environmental analyst Lester Brown, humans already demand that the planet regenerates its natural resources by 30% more than what is possible.[3] This is unsustainable.

Zoom in again on the forest and you can see the people involved: the employees at the logging and paper companies and quite possibly indigenous people to the area. Notice that the workers are employed (hopefully happily) by a company and are paid wages for their efforts. Optimistically, they make a living wage to cover their bills, are treated fairly, and are guaranteed some level of safety at work, which means they are given proper safety equipment (hard hats and clothing) that protect them from the weather and their working environment and are allowed time to take a break, relax, and eat. All of this food and equipment are also produced, sold, and delivered to stores and finally to the worker for consumption. As you can see, the economy and the interconnected components of the graphic design profession alone are complex.

Before we leave this example, however, zoom in a couple more times in the forest when the trees are being cut down. When a gas-powered saw or vehicle is turned on or when a tree falls, carbon dioxide is released into the atmosphere. This contributes to the already large amounts of greenhouse gases floating in the air and one of their impacts: global warming. Furthermore, each tree is home to other biological ecosystems of mammals, birds, amphibians, insects, and fungi. From our chapter title, the squirrel and the hawk, like other animals, rely on trees for shelter and food. Losing their homes means they must adapt or perish. Trees, besides most importantly producing oxygen we need to breathe, are also important to slow erosion, clean the air and soil, absorb carbon dioxide, and protect and shelter other fauna and flora in the forest. Paper manufacturers and the lumber industry in general find themselves under great economic, governmental, or social pressure to mitigate the negative impacts caused by logging practices. In response, many of these organizations affiliate with third-party forestry certification programs like the Forest Stewardship Council (FSC) or The Programme for the Endorsement of Forest Certification (PEFC) and engage in more sustainable forestry practices to balance consumer demand with preserving a healthy forest. Paper companies have had various levels of success globally in improving old practices in North America and Europe but have made only mixed progress in Asia, Africa, and South America.

To remedy past mistakes, many in the paper industry have also adopted sustainability principles that include protecting old growth trees, avoiding clear cutting, and the planting of new trees—but not necessarily the same species of tree that was cut down. This is an issue that can create problems for the ecosystem where the original tree once stood. Not all trees are created equal when it comes to who they best provide shelter and food for. So even tree planting, as necessary as it is, needs to be thought about in systems as well. Biodiversity is another key component of a living system.

Beyond the forest, there are other components of the paper supply chain: pulping, printing, distribution, use, and disposal with impacts and various levels of complexity in each step. Even digital design has some of the same components of the paper system like distribution, use, and disposal but is unique in other ways. There are the server farms that require great amounts of energy to run the machines that hold their petabytes of data. Energy is also used in manufacturing these machines. And don't forget the world of digital crosses paths with the realm of paper quite often. Designers rely on laptops and desktops to design things that will be printed, hosted, or cut from other materials like plastics and wood. The files are transferred through FTP or other cloud services to commercial printers who then use large digital or offset machines to print on the paper a designer has chosen. People also print information from the web which can be less wasteful if an efficient way to print is designed into the process.

After we zoom in to see the sum of its parts, the field of graphic design is clearly much bigger (and always expanding) than what's visible at first glance. So designers must look deeper because there can be a disconnect between the chosen materials and their place of origin. The journey from natural resource extraction through manufacturing and delivery of the final product is not as transparent as it should be. Much of what happens before that paper (or other material) is delivered is hidden from view. However knowing where the materials come from, how they're made, and how they get from there to here will help designers develop a more responsible and ethical outcome.

## SYSTEMS THINKING STRATEGIES

So what basic strategies can be used to quickly begin using systems thinking in the design practice? To begin, let's revisit design education and visualize the design process as a simple inverted pyramid divided into four parts (Figure 2.3). Historically, the focus in this process is to connect with the audience(s) and recognize the goals of the client. In the 2002 book *Cradle to Cradle*, architect William McDonough and chemist Michael Braungart describe this practice of designing and manufacturing as "...focused on making a product and getting it to a customer quickly and cheaply without considering much else."[4] Learning from what we've covered so far in this book, this aspect of the design process needs to shift to improve the triple bottom line and renourish what is taken away. However, the "inverted pyramid" design process does not need to be drastically altered or scrapped altogether. Instead, the standard four phases (research, ideation, refinement, and delivery) can remain but the funnel form (pyramid) is converted into a more woven circular structure. In this new shape, each phase informs one another and is interdependent on the one that is before or after. Despite keeping similar phases, the process works differently. Systems thinking suggests using what Fritjof Capra calls the "language of nature" as a model to look backward, forward, and dig deeper into a past project or phase for guidance. In other words, as designers, we must better understand how biological systems work and follow their lead in our decision-making processes. This is called biomimicry where designers use nature as a guide to create. In systems thinking, biomimicry is deeply embedded in the entire process of designing artifacts that follow a living cycle of balanced stocks (resources) and flows (manufacture and regrowth).

But how is designing in systems different in its process within this woven circular model? Designing using systems thinking is most successful when there is a clear project goal and you understand the relationships of the elements and connected impacts within the systems. So, instead of using only the inverted pyramid

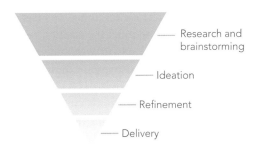

—— Research and brainstorming

—— Ideation

—— Refinement

—— Delivery

Figure 2.3 The inverted pyramid design process.

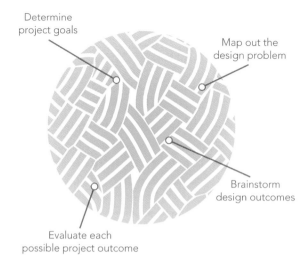

Determine
project goals

Map out the
design problem

Brainstorm
design outcomes

Evaluate each
possible project outcome

**Figure 2.4** Systems thinking process.

design approach, the systems design process involves four interlaced steps: determine project goals, map out the design problem, brainstorm design outcomes, and finally evaluate each possible project outcome. Compare that to the inverted pyramid and you can see that researching, ideating, refining, and delivering are all still part of our daily work, however renamed and integrated into a more cyclical and woven process. This new shape allows designers to work forward and backward (Figure 2.4), weaving in and out rather than in a linear progression as new developments and advancements in one area may affect and inform previously mapped out ideas and information in another. Working this way will allow for the concept and project to evolve holistically. Similar to the Powers of Ten, zooming into each element and relationship will help determine the impacts and potential for success when it comes to a more sustainable outcome.

## Determine project goals

This is the first crucial step to design in systems successfully. Here, the team determines the purpose of the project and eventually what it affects and how it will have impact. Without the collective comprehension of what the client truly needs, we all know, the results can miss the mark and be ineffective in achieving project goals as in the previous direct mail example. In meetings with the client, the initial conversation should not be about the solution or what is being made, but instead about understanding the needs, desires, and values of the audience(s). What is the problem to be solved? It's also important to identify past successes, pitfalls, and establish a means to measure each. Does this "conversation mapping" take up more time in the design process? It may or may not depending on the complexity of the project and to what extent the team is already in the research and discovery phase of their design process. You may find that the process consumes more time initially, but it results in an effective outcome that eliminates the need for a time-consuming and costly secondary solution or "fix."

After the client discussion, the designer and the team should have a crystal clear idea of what the design problem is and what it is connected to. Usually, the results of a client meeting would be in the form of a shared and agreed upon written project or creative brief that the audiences' values and triple bottom line goals— except with systems thinking, the solution is removed from the document. Doing so avoids limiting the design outcome and allows for a much deeper exploration of the problem, resulting in creative solutions. Much of what is in this document could be very different from what the client wanted going into the conversations. Sometimes, changing a client's perspective on something as supposedly simple as a color can be a challenge, so altering the entire scope of a project, one could imagine, could be quite a serious undertaking. If needed, even as daunting as this task this might be, it's useful and necessary. As you might have experienced many times, client expectations can be unrealistic and unfortunately uninformed. This is when it is necessary to switch into your educator hat; it will come in handy throughout the phases of a project.

## Map out the design problem

After the project brief, it's important to create a list or map of the design problems and how the audiences are connected or affected by each. Remember thinking in systems is about understanding project impacts holistically and not just independently. To start this step, it's helpful to find a large drawing surface like a whiteboard or chalkboard so that multiple people are able to participate easily and quickly. You can start simply by listing the design problem(s) on one side and the audience(s) in the middle. Draw lines to show connections from design problem(s) to an audience. Sticky notes are also useful so that pieces are easily repositioned and can be used to write smaller, detailed information. The idea is to sketch rapidly, erase, rearrange, brainstorm, and discuss. Using a computer to make a systems map is not ideal as this usually requires one person "driving" with multiple people acting as "backseat drivers." Mapping effectively requires all hands on deck.

Now you are ready to determine the relationships and boundaries of the audiences in the project. Creating user personas, as often done in User Interface (UI) and User Experience (UX) design, can be helpful for keeping the project and ideas focused and effective. Involving people from the community where the project will be implemented is always the best practice when developing user personas, but this is not always possible. Often designers rely on market research and interviews or information provided by the client. Some customer demographics will have overlapping needs and connections despite great differences in culture, gender, and geography, which is why creating user personas can help your team design to communicate effectively with the correct people.

At this point, you are only mapping the design problem and how the audiences are affected (Figure 2.5). In the next phase, solutions and other people are mapped into the system like the vendors who will help with implementation. The map will be fairly basic at this point in the process; however, more layers and details will be

Figure 2.5 Basic systems thinking map.

added along the way. The act of creating this map tasks us to look deeper into the design problems, who the audiences are, and how they are connected. As visual thinkers, designing this map of interconnections will only help designers see the beginning of the system more clearly. As you move into the next step, you should begin to think about documenting all of these elements in the context where this project exists. Could it be in a commercial or community space?, Both?, Will it require more partners to help complete?

## Brainstorm design outcomes

With the basic systems map containing audiences and design problems in hand, it's time to brainstorm ways to solve the design dilemma. The clear understanding of the project goals, the audience needs, the diversity of the audience's cultural experiences, and how they are all connected are combined together to help you develop possible solutions for improving the triple bottom line. The ideal goal again is a living cycle where waste equals food. The beginning part of this phase is one we are all are familiar with; what needs to be created and why? Should this be print or digital? Both? Some hybrid solution connected to a service or something unexpected? The potential solutions you find most interesting and effective in solving the design problem should be layered on to the systems map.

What does it mean to map solutions? To begin with, define possible physical or digital outcomes of each design problem and place it within the system. Here again you can connect design problems with outcomes and ask what audience(s) would best relate to which solution? In answering that question, connect possible outcomes with audiences and then detail out that relationship(s). For instance, think back to the triple bottom line—people, planet, and profit. With each potential outcome and connected audience further questions should be asked like, "will this outcome be cost effective for the client and audience(s)?" What will each solution be made from? Will the materials needed for the outcome require shipping or manufacture from overseas? Here, we are focusing on the profit component of the triple bottom line and describing how each solution can be effective with the systems of audiences and be economically viable as well (Figure 2.6). List them out on the map. This step will run smoother with color coding. Whether it be sticky notes or markers/pencils, assigning colors to connected design problems or audiences as well as differentiating positive from negative impacts will help you and your team read the map more easily and quickly.

## Evaluate each possible project outcome

This is the most detailed and challenging of all the four phases. Again, we will need to embrace the concept of the powers of ten. In each of the previous project outcomes on the map, it is important now to delve deeper into their impacts outside of just the financial or usability ones. Connecting back to the triple bottom line, this fourth stage focuses not only on the "planet" component but also on "people" and "profit" once environmental impacts are learned. Again, systems thinking is not about isolating and exploring one element of a system, instead it's about understanding how the elements in the project are interconnected and why.

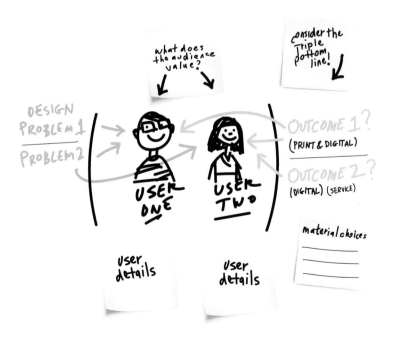

Figure 2.6 More detailed systems thinking map.

The woven circle model is a nice visual to describe systems thinking when it comes to design. Despite a phased-based design process, while thinking in systems, we are most importantly "weaving" back and forth between the phases as much as we are zooming into the details to better understand what project outcome will best benefit the client and have the most positive effects on the triple bottom line. It may be necessary to revisit and modify previous decisions after making discoveries in these later steps.

With each potential project outcome that was determined in the previous phase, you defined the basic materials needed and how each part of the project will impact the audience(s). In this phase, the team must now resolve how the material choices will have effects on the environment. List the materials you plan to use (plastic(s), paper, paperboard, etc.) for each outcome and dig into where and how they are manufactured. In this research, you should also choose vendors and know their locations to add to the map (Figure 2.7).

Obviously, the integral part of material choice is where it is sourced from, its impact, and overall sustainability. Graphic designers should aim here to choose

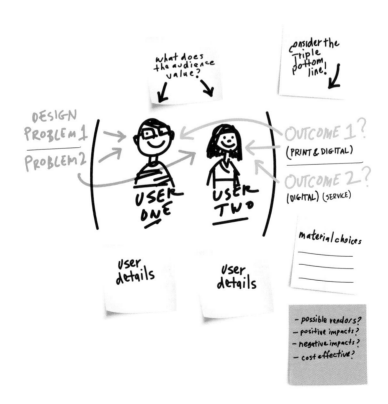

Figure 2.7 Final systems thinking map.

vendors located close to one another (if something is being manufactured), near distribution centers, that use renewable energy, have trusted social and environmental certifications, and use post-consumer waste materials. In general, using virgin materials (even those which are certified) will have a greater negative impact on the air, land, and water than those that are from post-consumer supplies. Post-consumer, agricultural waste, and recycled materials, like paper or paperboard, tap into a waste stream and prevent discarded paper and other materials from heading to the landfill, require less energy and water to manufacture, emit less greenhouse gases in production, and help in the effort to prevent deforestation. In fact, for example, with paper, each ton of 100% recycled fiber that displaces a ton of virgin fiber saves about 24 trees.[5] As part of this decision-making, ensuring you reduce material usage is always important.

Even more exciting is the idea of collecting agricultural residues (leftover stalks of corn, wheat straw, etc., from harvest) to manufacture paper and paper products. If you recall from the Introduction, our goal was to print this book on paper made primarily from wheat straw. With these types of papers, designers' reliance on trees is reduced (needed in our quest to slow global warming), using the agricultural waste stream to make a better compostable product instead. It is important to note, however, that the bulk of the leftover corn stalks and wheat straw is needed by the soil for nutrition (like the oak tree needs its fallen leaves), so we cannot take all of this crop residue to fulfill our needs. In a 2006 study by the United States Department of Agriculture (USDA) on biofuels, it was found that up to 30% of the corn stalk remnants could be used without harming the soil nutrition.[6] It's a sign again that it's best to design following our biological systems as a guide. As McDonough and Braungart state, "waste equals food."

To truly quantify the environmental and social impacts of graphic design work would require a life cycle analysis (LCA). Performing a LCA requires money, time, and outside scientific partners. This is not something designers are necessarily trained to do or have the equipment to do quickly, but it is recommended and hopefully will become accessible to all designers in the near future. However, in general, designing to minimize material, waste, distance traveled for distribution, and working with vendors that utilize renewable energy will reduce negative impacts. Those are basic strategies to remember but not the only ones to keep top of mind. Beyond specifying alternative, recycled, or post-consumer waste materials there are a number of different yet connected variables need to be explored. How can you reduce material use and design efficiently to maximize the materials you are using? Where are the vendors located? Are these vendors close to the resources being used in the project and to the distribution centers to cut back on the transportation emissions? Zooming into the systems map here allows for a look into these smaller but important connections which really do make a great impact on the planet.

For instance, it may be cheaper to print or purchase materials internationally instead of regionally, but besides the short-term economic benefits, what are the other long-term impacts? By using systems thinking, it becomes clear that there can be greater greenhouse gas emissions in shipping/distribution and less environmental and social oversights to the final outcome. This is not desirable. There are more stringent and significant standards and certifications that North American and European printers must adhere to in comparison with some other countries. These standards and certifications help ensure fair wage and safety practices for their employees. This is not insinuating that every non-Western vendor doesn't care for or pay fair wages to their workers, but certifications like Occupational Safety and Health Administration (OSHA), International Organization for Standardization (ISO), Better Business Bureau (BBB), B Corporation, and the Consumer Product Safety Commission (CPSC) guarantee legal and measurable benefits to employees, and these certifications are found more regularly in North America and Europe. Sustainability is also about justice. Clean air, water, and land combined with safe working conditions and equitable wage practices will create a thriving system. In nature, when there are more hawks than squirrels, there is less food and consequently a disruption in the food chain which creates inequity and, in turn, starvation. Comparably, less regulations on safety will lead to accidents, health hazards, worker frustration, and potentially protests creating a public relations nightmare and leading to economic disruption for the company. Respecting and emulating biological systems are the best ways to operate, and supporting vendors that use fair practices is ideal for healthy people, planet, and economy.

When zooming in on the impacts to the triple bottom line of each possible project outcome, it is very likely you will stumble upon questions that you are unable to answer. For example, in the process of writing and planning for the production for this book, we also ran into moments where we were lost for answers. To remedy this, we called in experts on paper, printing, and the environment. Thinking in systems means understanding the design problem as a whole and this includes, of course, connecting with our collaborators. By reaching out to people who knew more than us on environmental policies, printing, and energy, we were able to present solutions to our design problems with this book and work toward the most responsible production approach possible. This strategy is imperative with implementing systems thinking effectively in one's work. Designers cannot be experts in everything; therefore, it is wise to seek out specialists when researching materials and processes whenever necessary. Designers are not going to change the paradigm alone—allies and partners must do so together. However, it is true that individually each designer can make positive impacts with more informed and responsible decisions.

It is also important to note that by taking a deeper look into the system, problems can be located before they happen. Through the sharing of knowledge and ideation through collaboration, graphic designers can work to develop effective, sustainable solutions appropriate to the culture and environment in which projects will be implemented. Just like with the *Gestalt* theory we referred to earlier, any impact on one part of a design impacts the whole; it's important to be mindful of how the impacts from a single decision affect other parts of the system from the people in the supply chain, to the animal habitats affected by the materials sourcing, to the financial limitations of the intended consumer. A decision on any part of a design requires that a balance process be in place for all other affected parts. The question of "which option meets the client's needs while having the greatest positive impacts?" is one that should be asked at all times during this fourth phase using your increasingly complex looking map of elements, interactions, and outcomes as your guide.

## GROWING FORWARD

This augmentation to the design process we present is a practice, like your own interests and techniques, in a state of growth and flux. We recognize the need for and encourage further experimentation with systems thinking strategies within this profession we care so much about. One aspect which needs more thought is that of "giving back" or "to renourish" during and after this design process. In our earlier examples in this chapter, we described methods to reduce the impact but not improve the world around us through design. This is clearly something that must be done considering the rate at which society is gobbling up natural resources and exacerbating the current and future negative impacts of global warming. Not cutting down trees, switching to a waste stream of agricultural fibers for paper, and using renewable energy can be net zero activities, but a net positive activity is very much necessary. William McDonough and Michael Braungart call this the "upcycle" or adding "...value by transforming or reinventing an otherwise-disposable item into something of higher quality."[7] Planting considerably more trees than what is used; improving living conditions and socioeconomic standings; and restoring air, water, and soil to cleaner states are all examples of renourishing our world. However, currently, this way of creating is not taught in most schools (K-12 and higher education) or practiced consistently within the corporate world. Instead, how humanity lives on the planet is in stark contrast to this model of renourishing.

It is our hope that by better understanding and embracing how the biological systems of the planet operate, change can be brought about in how people live and design. Making decisions to reduce impact is good; however, what has been damaged by our collective actions must be repaired. To think in systems means acknowledging that humans are only a small part of the huge web of life and depend on nature's fruits for the freedoms they need and enjoy. In other words, we see ourselves not only as designers but also as human beings reliant on a much larger natural series of connected systems. "Seeing the whole" is the only ethical and just strategy for designing going forward. Patrice Martin from IDEO.org agrees, "(d)esign can change the world because it gets us to new answers and we desperately need new answers."[8] We urge you to seek new answers—to go outside and observe for yourself. You'll be surprised by the inspiration everywhere when you stop to not just smell but watch the roses. In the next sections of the book, we will see some inspiring, in-depth graphic design case studies that use systems thinking for sustainable results.

## ENDNOTES

1. Muir, John. *My First Summer in the Sierra.* Boston, MA: Houghton Mifflin, 1911. 110.
2. "Response Rate 2012 Report: Data to Benchmark All Your Marketing Campaigns." *Direct Marketing Association.* January 1, 2012. Accessed February 26, 2015.
3. Brown, Lester. "Selling Our Future." In *Plan B 4.0: Mobilizing to Save Civilization*, 15. New York: W. W. Norton, 2009.
4. McDonough, William, and Michael Braungart. *Cradle to Cradle: Remaking the Way We Make Things.* New York: North Point Press, 2002. 26.
5. Depending, of course, on the size of the tree. Kinsella, Susan. "Paperwork: Comparing Recycled to Virgin Paper." *Environmental Paper Network.* April 1, 2002. http://environmentalpaper.org/wp-content/uploads/2012/02/Paperwork.pdf. Accessed February 12, 2015.
6. Andrews, Susan. "Crop Residue Removal for Biomass Energy Production: Effects on Soils and Recommendations." *USDA-Natural Resource Conservation Service.* February 22, 2006. http://www.nrcs.usda.gov/Internet/FSE_DOCUMENTS/nrcs142p2_053255.pdf. Accessed February 12, 2015.
7. McDonough, William, and Michael Braungart. *The Upcycle: Beyond Sustainability—Designing for Abundance.* New York: North Point Press, 2013.
8. "The Human Center of Design: In Conversation with IDEO.org's Patrice Martin." *Impact Design Hub.* July 08, 2015. https://impactdesignhub.org/2015/07/08/human-center-of-design-ideoorg-patrice-martin/#c77-blog.

# Chapter 3
## A CLEAR PICTURE

When we were planning this book, we came across several publications, case studies, and articles with examples of finished and theoretical design projects but found very little transparency with regard to how the case studies were chosen. This was somewhat surprising. Today, everything from business practices to personal behavior is open to public scrutiny, especially on social media, which provide everyone a voice and a platform (for better or for worse). Organizations must now more than ever be transparent and ethical as these qualities are essential for fair business and for building trust. Go search #greenwashing on Twitter and you will scroll through countless instances where companies are publicly called out for dishonest declarations of corporate responsibility. Graphic designers, of course, have a part to play in that. Designers and businesses must demonstrate trust together by providing the details of the safety, environmental impact, and benefits of the project to the users. We wanted to promote this principle, and knew you would be curious, so we included our set of selection criteria for all case studies featured in this book.

The questions we asked each designer or team are a part of our process for designing using systems thinking explained in the previous chapter. For example, we wanted to know how the design team guided the project thinking about the triple bottom line, the client's goals, and if there were financial and time constraints. We also asked what challenges were faced, how they were overcome, and finally in hindsight what could have been done differently to make the outcome even more sustainable. In addition to these questions, we also asked what materials were used, how waste and energy were minimized or eliminated, and what certifications the materials and vendors maintained to ensure that the triple bottom line was considered throughout the entire supply chain of manufacture and delivery. These are the same inquiries that we consistently undertake as we approach our own work and research, ensuring we exceed best practices and find new and innovative ways to incorporate systems thinking. We will wax philosophic about this in Chapter 6 of this book, which is inspired by the lessons learned from the case studies in Chapter 4.

We also felt that it was extremely important to include case studies that provided realistic paths forward to design more sustainably along with details and reflections from the designers or the team that made it all possible. That type of information will serve as the best practices we consistently aim for in our own work and present on our site www.re-nourish.org. These methods can be a catalyst for increased momentum toward a more sustainable graphic design profession. We are always upbeat for a better today and tomorrow when we come across the case studies you will see in the next chapters but are frustrated, like many of you, about the pace at which the profession is adopting and implementing sustainable design practices with clients. Hopefully, these case studies will help speed up that dialogue and practical application. This is one of our many goals in writing this book.

Another aspect that we found curiously missing from the case studies in the books that came before ours was clear standards for inclusion into the publication. As interior design and architecture adopted LEED (Leadership in Energy and Environmental Design) certification in the mid-1990s as a method to better quantify the environmental benefits of building with more sustainable regional materials and designing for energy/water efficiency, we felt a similar model should be used not only to select the case studies for the book but also for the sustainability of the profession. By using a transparent selection criteria for how the case studies were chosen help provide a measurable barometer as to what makes a graphic design project more sustainable. That information can be used as the starting point to design more responsibly.

## A CONFUSION OF CERTIFICATION

Without clear guidelines, how, then, do we determine sustainability in graphic design? At times, it can be difficult to judge when one choice is more or less sustainable than another. To confuse things, recent popularity of greener options globally has led to "greenwashing," where misleading or false claims of environmental friendliness have puzzled consumers. The term greenwashing is derived from the words "green" (environmentally sound) and "whitewashing" (to conceal or gloss over wrongdoing) and is applied when companies or their products are marketed to appear more environmentally sound than they really are. This has led to skepticism about eco-friendly claims and a dilution of the importance of sustainability. Because greenwashing is so prevalent, extra diligence is needed during research and decision-making to determine the most responsible materials and vendors. Among the many areas designers should pay close attention, this is particularly true when choosing paper.

Although marketed as the most environment-friendly option, recycled tree fiber may not always be the ideal choice when it comes to paper (although if you are reading a paper version of this book, you are, in fact, holding 30% post-consumer tree fiber. And if you skipped over the Introduction (no!), go back and give it a read—we've spelled out how this book was made). Although seldom promoted, paper made from agricultural residue is the most sustainable option when considering the "ingredients" alone. This type of paper is made from the unused remains of food crops (like wheat) rather than plants specifically grown to make paper products (like bamboo). The stalks that remain from food crops are often discarded and burned, releasing carbon dioxide and creating air pollution. Paper made from agricultural residue can reduce both and save trees by replacing wood fiber for making paper.

However, choosing agricultural-residue paper also requires looking at other connected factors. As thinking in systems reveals, there are many considerations when choosing paper, like where the paper is manufactured and how far it needs to be shipped. Designers must also take into account where the fiber was harvested, if it was bleached, if the paper was manufactured with renewable energy, if the company's employment practices are fair, and how the company impacts the surrounding communities or treats its employees. That's a lot of "ifs" and also a dizzying amount of information to research that can be accessible only through more corporate transparency. Certifications and standards can be important tools in this equation and are helpful to get the entire view of the triple bottom line. However, a product or material's lack of certifications does not always indicate that a business is unsustainable or unethical. Applying for certifications can be too costly for small businesses even if they have already employed responsible environmental and social practices. So however ideal a particular paper may appear, sometimes the shipping distance or a company's treatment of its employees makes it a less sustainable choice than the one sourced more regionally or from a company that pays a living wage. Weighing the options and looking at all the connected concerns help to make more informed decisions for sustainable outcomes.

## PRINT VERSUS DIGITAL

We are often asked if digital solutions are more sustainable than print. The answer to this question is quite convoluted. Sometimes, it is best to create a digital outcome, while other times, printing may be more effective in communicating the message. Considerations for choosing the right medium depend on the audience, participants, distribution area, materials, and vendors. Digital-only solutions, although they reduce paper use and transportation, may not be the ideal choice if the hosting company or data farm is powered by fossil fuels or conducts unfair labor practices for example.

The computers and other electronics necessary for digital work also become an environmental and human health hazard at the end of their lifecycles. It is important to point out that this same problem exists in print design. Graphic designers use digital devices in the process of developing printed outcomes. Large- and small-scale printers, desktop and laptop computers, scanners, and digital cameras also end up in the landfill or are exported for dangerous disassembly overseas. Whether the end result is print or digital, hours are spent researching online, creating mockups, e-mailing, writing, sending files, and working in the cloud. Whether or not the work is finished at the digital stage, or the files are sent off to a printer, working on screen is embedded in almost all of graphic design. It's critical when deciding between digital and print to look at the entire system in which your piece will live and die. Mapping out all the possible solutions and connected impacts is the best process to determine what to implement and why.

Digital or print, sustainable graphic design goes beyond a material choice or a web hosting decision. It must take into consideration all the places where project decisions make an impact, and instead of trying to only mitigate the negative impacts, design can be produced to have a positive, nourishing effect on the environment, people, and the economy. This is sustainable graphic design and what the profession should ideally strive for.

## OUR STANDARDS

Through research of industry and environmental statistics and trends, we developed a set of standards for Re-nourish that we used to judge the credibility of the case study submissions for this book. Most importantly, our standards imply that prior to the launch of any design project all the players involved spend time thinking about the triple bottom line and the impacts of their decisions. The standards on our site are not a certification by any means, instead a logical set of tiered benchmarks for continued improvement toward a triple bottom line approach to graphic design. With this assurance that specific criteria have been met and verified, designers can have the power to demonstrate sustainability efforts, facilitating the implementation of more sustainable design practices to clients and throughout the industry.

We not only used these standards as the goal but also accepted specific case studies that strived to be as sustainable as possible. The goal of the project should not merely be to find a solution that harms less but rather to improve the world through its creation. This is a challenging but attainable objective. All together, the case studies tell a story—one that is exciting and inspiring for the journey forward.

The Re-nourish standards for print/packaging or digital are divided into sections that detail specifics on materials, production, energy, process, and end-of-life cycle. On our website, we have subdivided each type of design outcome (print or digital) into tiers that mimic the structure used by architects (LEED) for ease of understanding and also to help motivate all of us to keep pushing toward the highest ideal level of sustainable design. For this book, we didn't categorize each case study using the tier-based system from our site in order to flatten the process, instead we chose the projects that reached closest to the optimum (tier one).

In our call for case study submissions, we chose the most relevant questions from our site's existing standards questionnaire to build the most interesting story for each example. As we believe in full transparency, we have included the full list of criteria used to select the case studies in each project outcome category:

*Source materials:*
- The major material components for the project are compostable biodegradable resins, or regional agri-fiber or agricultural residue (wheat straw, corn stover, hemp, kenaf, begasse, prairie grasses, etc.), or 100% recycled material.

- Recyclable, reclaimed, and safer industrial materials (steel, aluminum, tin) that can be used for re-manufacture.
- Regional to the determined vendors.
- Manufactured by renewable energy (or less preferably, with renewable energy credits).
- Sourcing does not compromise local communities or harm biological systems.

*Design:*
- Easily disassembled (for multiple parts).
- Recyclable.
- No adhesives.
- Designed to minimize the amount of materials used (efficient use of the press sheet— rightsized and limited print runs).
- Minimize tertiary packaging (maximize amount of product shipped at once).
- Primary and secondary packaging must work together to reduce space and materials.
- Designed for intentional reuse and end-of-life material recovery or compostable.
- Digital projects have print-friendly options when applicable.
- Digital projects must meet accessibility guidelines as set forth by the World Wide Web Consortium (W3C) where applicable, like cross-browser and platform compatibility and accessibility (i.e., Alt text for images, transcripts for podcasts, closed captions for video/animation, and keyboard input).
- Web-based projects minimize file sizes and use optimized and efficient coding strategies (HTML, CSS, and JavaScript minification) to reduce loading time.

*Project messaging:*
- The project must not impede basic human rights or be designed so as to negatively impact the biological environment.
- Must not knowingly communicate false claims or untruthful information.
- Environmental message (eco-audit or encouragement of reuse/recycle) on printed or digital outcome.

*Inks:*
- Vegetable-based inks with low volatile organic compounds.
- Less than 30% ink coverage and no bleeds.
- No metallic inks or foils, varnishes, laminates, and ultraviolet coatings (aqueous coatings, embossing, die cuts, and engravings are acceptable).

*Design studio/agency:*
- Files are transmitted online.
- Project is proofed onscreen as much as possible.
- Nonvital long distance client meetings are held virtually.
- Provides pro-bono work for, or donates to, charitable causes.

*Design studio/agency and vendor practices:*

- Have formal waste reduction/recycling policies in operation.
- Formal eco-preferable purchasing policies in operation.
- Pays local living wages and offers employee health insurance and benefits.
- Offers employee incentives for using public transportation, walking, or biking to work.

*Design studio/agency and vendor energy and equipment:*

- Hosting and/or data farms for design studio and client work are powered by 100% renewable energy (solar, wind, geothermal, etc.).
- Office/studio/business is powered by 100% renewable energy (solar, wind, geothermal, etc.).
- Formal energy reduction policy in operation.
- Utilizes equipment that is Energy Star rated (or internationally equivalent).
- Formal electronics recycling or donation policies in operation.

**Note:** The following case studies vary in both design process and outcomes, and also provide diverse examples in response to the different cultures where the projects are based. Where it makes sense, we have included lessons learned and areas for further exploration and opportunities. Most importantly, we hope these case studies will provide inspiration and serve as invaluable examples of how you can realistically incorporate systems thinking to improve the triple bottom line in your own upcoming design projects.

# Chapter 4

## CASE STUDIES

**Modern Species**

Seattle, WA, USA

www.modernspecies.com

**Creative Director**

Gage Mitchell

**Designer**

Gage Mitchell

**Copywriter**

Lisa Brill

**Copy Editor**

Jennifer Stewart

CLIENT

**Qet® Botanicals**

Cross Plains, WI, USA

www.qetbotanicals.com

## About Modern Species

Modern Species is a sustainable branding and graphic design studio helping natural and organic product companies move their mission forward. We work with passionate people, both entrepreneurs and in-house teams, to help focus their vision and then make their dream a reality with beautiful print, packaging, and digital experiences. By consistently focusing on the economy, environment, and ethics, we're able to help good companies fulfill their brand promises and increase their positive impact in their community and beyond. We do all of this because we believe that a more beautiful, functional, and sustainable world is a goal worth pursuing.

## What were the project goals?

Qet approached Modern Species with an idea for a skin care company comprising products made from only the purest, freshest organic botanical ingredients.

They had a name and most of the product formulas but needed a brand, website, packaging, and sales collateral to get their vision off the napkin and into the market. As a small company launching with nearly 40 stock keeping units (SKUs), we had to find a way for Qet's brand and package to make a big splash without piling up too much debt. Therefore, sustainability wasn't only important to their ethos, but it also had the potential to stretch their start-up budget further, allowing them to launch a full line of products on day one. Although the entire project would be great to dissect, this case study will focus on the packaging (Figures 4.1 through 4.6).

We worked closely with the founders for about 10 months, first establishing the brand platform, setting a goal for the visuals, and then working through the design process on each deliverable from concept to launch. At each step, we continually asked ourselves how the ideas bubbling up might impact the environment, how it would impact the financial bottom line of the company (and thereby the sales price of the products), and how our choices might affect people and cultures along the supply chain.

## Were the sustainable parameters for this project introduced by Qet, Modern Species, or both?

The parameters for the packaging were minimal. We had a basic idea of what packaging forms Qet would use and the range of sizes that would fit the 40 SKUs, but beyond that, we were all open to letting the right solution be uncovered by the design process. Sustainability was a must, of course, and a priority on both sides, but how that expressed itself was yet to be determined.

## How did you guide Qet to the best possible solution to improve the triple bottom line?

After researching the industry and finding a lot of wasted material with excessively large (and often redundant) boxes that held small bottles, we realized that

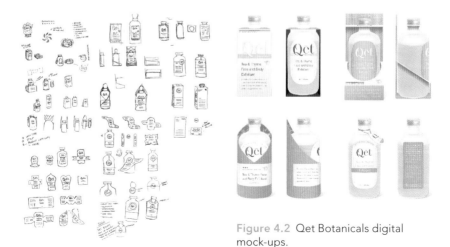

Figure 4.2 Qet Botanicals digital mock-ups.

Figure 4.1 Qet Botanicals sketches.

Figure 4.3  Qet Botanicals product line.

Figure 4.4  Qet Botanicals half-box.

finding the right label and box system was a great place to focus our sustainability efforts. Through a series of conceptual explorations we came up with a range of ideas for solving this problem that included ideas like hang tags, unfolding labels, and right-sized boxes. One of the ideas we ended up pitching to Qet was a half-box that would show off the product and save a ton of money by reducing materials and eliminating some of the finishing work and glues. Lisa, the founder of Qet, fell in love with the idea and we ended up choosing that direction to push forward. Throughout the rest of the process, we worked closely with Qet to make triple bottom line decisions like ethical paper sourcing, renewable and renewed materials, cost-saving methods of press sheet optimization, and much more.

Figure 4.5  Qet Botanicals half-box.

Figure 4.6  Qet Botanicals product line.

What challenges did you encounter when trying to design the packaging in the most sustainable way possible? How did you overcome those challenges?

We wanted to find a way to eliminate the boxes all together but found there was no way to fit all the necessary information on the smaller bottles. We thought about a hangtag, but that took up too much shelf space and was practically the same size as the smallest bottle. So, instead, we came up with the half-box design to wrap around the smaller bottles as a great compromise between all products that have full boxes or no boxes at all.

Finding the right half-box design, paper weight, and lock-tab system to eliminate the need for glues and have the box securely fasten onto the bottles was a bit of a struggle that we were eventually able to overcome with the help of our printer, DCG ONE. We also had to ensure that eliminating the protective boxes wouldn't make bulk shipping too difficult, but Qet found that by reusing the boxes that the bottles and jars came in, they were able to ship the products safely in bulk.

For the labels, we used TerraSkin, which is a tree-free stone "paper" that requires no water to manufacture, would recycle easily with the glass bottles, and holds up against the essential oils in the skincare products.

How did you design the packaging to minimize materials?

By taking a strip of paper and die cutting a hole for the neck of the bottle and some lock-tabs, we were able to make a "box" that securely wraps around the smaller products vertically, giving us the extra label space we needed while showing off the product, reducing material usage, and eliminating the need for glues. These half-boxes gang up a press sheet nicely, since they're simple strips of paper. They also ship efficiently since they have no glue and can lay flat. Also, with the lock-tabs and bottle neck cut outs, we were able to eliminate the need for adhesives. After purchasing the product, the consumer can either undo the tuck-flaps or tear the box away and recycle it with paper.

Which aspect of the project met Qet's needs while having the greatest positive impacts on environmental, societal, cultural, and economic sustainability?

Although the entire brand launch was much bigger than just the packaging case study we're outlining here, the solution we came up with allowed Qet to launch with a full line of beautifully packaged products on a start-up budget and, compared with industry standard (excessive boxes), was able to do so with a much smaller environmental footprint. Beyond that, we were able to specify materials and vendors that support ethical sourcing and workplace conditions.

## Project Details

### HALF-BOX PAPER

**Mohawk Loop Smooth PC 100**

**Specs**
130# Cover
100% post-consumer waste

**Certifications**
Forest Stewardship Council (FSC)
Green Seal
Green-e
Processed chlorine-free (PCF)

### LABELS

**TerraSkin**

**Certifications**
Cradle to Cradle Silver Certified

### BOXES AND STATIONERY PRINTER

**DCG ONE**
Seattle, WA

**Certifications, partnerships, memberships**
FSC
EnviroStar
Green Power Partnership
3Degrees, Green Up

### LABELS PRINTER

**Richmark Label**
Seattle, WA

**Now that the project is complete, what would you have done differently to make the project more sustainable while still meeting the client's goals?**

Looking back on the project, we would have designed the labels differently to make them easier to print since we ended up having to reprint (waste of materials) many of the labels for quality reasons (the faded flower behind the type caused lots of problems). We would also go back and make the recycling instructions on the labels more specific to include information about the lids, which we now know more about.

**What advice do you have for designers just starting to integrate systems thinking into their client work?**

My best piece of advice for designers wanting to be more sustainable is to be curious. Asking yourself, and others, what happens to a package after the consumer is done with it, where and how materials are sourced, or how your solution will work at scale, for example, is a great way to learn where problems exist. Once you know where you can make a big impact, you can focus your design thinking on those issues to find better solutions to difficult problems. The more you learn about the system within which your design solution lives, the smarter your designs will be and the better you will serve your clients.

# SWERVE DESIGN GROUP:
## COMMUNICATING ACCESSIBILITY

**PROJECT CREDITS**

**Swerve Design Group**

Toronto, Ontario, Canada

www.swervedesign.com

**Creative Director**

David Johnson

**Art Director**

Mark Haak

**Designers**

Mark Haak and David Johnson

**CLIENT**

**Environmental Commissioner of Ontario**

Ontario, Canada

www.eco.on.ca

## About Swerve Design Group

Swerve Design Group specializes in creative graphic design and engaging online experiences that move people to action. Beyond Swerve's design work, their strategic process navigates a path and strategically steers clients toward their marketing destination.

## What were the project goals?

The Environmental Commissioner of Ontario (ECO) is the independent environmental watchdog of the province. We were asked to design a report for them that could be printed with high environmental standards and create online versions to increase access to the reports (Figures 4.7 through 4.10).

Figure 4.7  Environmental Commissioner of Ontario report cover.

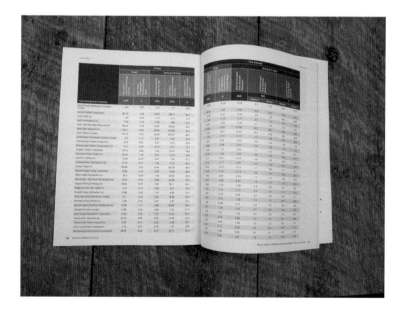

Figure 4.8  Environmental Commissioner of Ontario report interior spread 1.

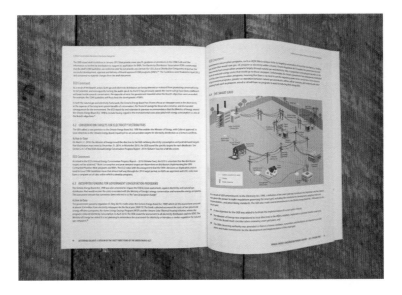

Figure 4.9 Environmental Commissioner of Ontario report interior spread 2.

### How did you guide ECO to the best possible solution to improve the triple bottom line?

The original scope of the project was to design a printed report and create a downloadable PDF for their website, but we identified an opportunity to make the report more accessible and encourage ECO to print less reports in the future by creating ePub versions optimized by tablet/mobile phone.

### What challenges did Swerve encounter when trying to design the project in the most sustainable way possible? How did you overcome those challenges?

The report has a lot of content, so it required a lot of pages to print. We worked to keep the page count as low as possible while still keeping the font sizes legible. We also printed separate English and French reports instead of combining them into one document so that we could reduce the print run by having a smaller run for the French version which had a smaller audience than the English version.

### How did the Swerve Design Group design the printed and digital report to minimize the use of resources?

We suggested the client consider ePub versions as a way to test the accessibility of the report with a future goal in mind to move away from printing the publication and go completely digital, if possible. In the print design, we set suitable margins, font sizes, and page layouts to minimize the number of pages that needed to be printed. The printing itself was done in the most environment-friendly way we could to save resources. The project was printed on Canadian-made Rolland Enviro 100 paper. Rolland Enviro 100 is made entirely from recycled paper fiber which saves the harvesting of mature trees, reduces solid waste that would have

Figure 4.10 Environmental Commissioner of Ontario digital report.

gone into landfills, uses 80% less water, resulting in less air and water pollution than conventional paper manufacturing. Rolland Enviro 100 is also made with biogas energy which is an alternative "green energy" source produced from decomposing waste collected from landfill sites.

**Which aspect of the project met the ECO's needs while having the greatest positive impacts on environmental, societal, cultural, and economic sustainability?**

The project was a huge success. The paper was sourced locally and FSC certified, processed chlorine-free with 100% post-consumer waste fiber, and manufactured with biogas energy. We also included paper-free ePub versions for interactive online viewing on iPads and other tablets and mobile phones. This allowed us to increase the reach of the publication without printing any additional reports and gave us the ability to monitor the success of the ePub version to help ECO

## Project Details

### PAPER

**Rolland Enviro 100**

### Specs

100% post-consumer waste

Made with biogas energy

### Certifications

Forest Stewardship Council (FSC)

Processed chlorine-free

EcoLogo

### PRINTER

**Warren's Waterless Printing**

Toronto, Ontario, Canada

### Certifications, partnerships, memberships

Forest Stewardship Council (FSC)

Ontario Environmental Leaders

ISO 14001

EcoLogo Environmental Choice Programs

move toward printing less reports in future years. We also recommended using Adobe InCopy for a more collaborative approach to editing copy and approvals which they now use as a standard on all their report processes.

**Now that the project is complete, what would you have done differently to make the project more sustainable while still meeting the client's goals?**

We would love to see the report go entirely digital.

**What advice do you have for designers just starting to integrate systems thinking into their client work?**

Think about the big picture—what is the primary goal and what is the best way to communicate that goal? What formats can we use that will use the least amount of resources? Are there better approaches to take? Question everything, challenge existing processes, and explore the best solutions to reach those goals.

# STUDIO EMMI: ENVIRONMENTAL GRAPHICS FOR ENVIRONMENTAL SUSTAINABILITY

## PROJECT CREDITS

**Studio EMMI**

London, UK

www.emmi.co.uk

### Creative Director

Emmi Salonen

### Designers

Emmi Salonen

## CLIENT

**Contemporary Art Archipelago**

Turku Archipelago, Finland

www.contemporaryartarchipelago.fi

## About Studio EMMI

EMMI set up her graphic design practice Studio EMMI in 2005. Studio EMMI designs identities, websites, catalogs, books, and environmental graphics. Over the years, we have developed a strong track record and a long list of happy clients from the worlds of art, culture, commerce, and academia. Said clients come in all shapes and sizes, but they are all brands with vitality, passion, and direction.

Studio EMMI has always had a keen interest in environmentally sound solutions. Besides designing, EMMI teaches at various UK universities and lectures regularly nationwide. She is the author of the book *Common Interest: Documents* and contributes to industry magazines on request (Figures 4.11 through 4.16).

Figure 4.11 Identity in use on the leaflet covers—English and Finnish leaflets. (Courtesy of Jere Salonen.)

Figure 4.12 Outdoor signage, caption for the site-specific art work. (Courtesy of Stefan Crämer.)

## What were the project goals?

The Contemporary Art Archipelago (CAA) exhibition consists of over 20 new, site-specific artworks and events realized in the Turku Archipelago in Finland by international and local artists during the Summer of 2011, between June 18 and September 30. CAA is encountered from cruise ships, small boats, along roads, virtually, on a remote islet, in the sea, on the airwaves, on the ferries, or even in a private home. The theme of the exhibition was the archipelago and its future as

Figure 4.13 Leaflet inner layout, showing minimal use of color. (Courtesy of Jere Salonen.)

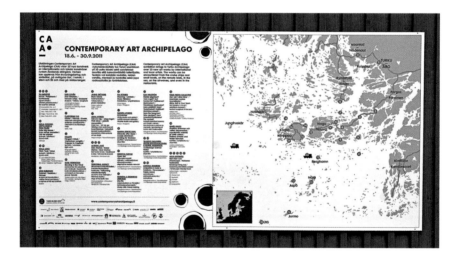

Figure 4.14 CAA location map, information graphics. (Courtesy of Stefan Crämer.)

a unique yet changing environment and mode of life. The context of the Baltic Sea was strongly present, yet CAA reflects the specificities of Turku Archipelago also against other similar environments and global changes. The artists examine, among others, alternative island lifestyles and livelihoods, transformations in ecological and cultural diversity, as well as desires projected onto islands and across the sea.

We were asked to create the overall identity and graphics for CAA. The identity spoke to art being entwined with its environment—the archipelago. The deliverables included identity, website, leaflets, posters, signage, maps, captions, ads, and a book.

Figure 4.15  Stationery design. (Courtesy of Jere Salonen.)

Figure 4.16  Outdoor sign, location mark. (Courtesy of Stefan Crämer.)

**Were the sustainable parameters for this project introduced by CAA, Studio EMMI, or both?**

We both together developed the sustainability parameters for this exciting project.

**How did you guide CAA to the best possible solution to improve the triple bottom line?**

In this project, the client was very keen to make everything as sustainable and environmentally friendly as possible in order to reflect the overall ethos of the art exhibition and commissions. We were lucky to have a wonderful client who did not need much guidance toward a more sustainable outcome.

**What challenges did you encounter when trying to design the exhibition in the most sustainable way possible? How did you overcome those challenges?**

The biggest challenge was that each leaflet and connected item had to be in three different languages: Finnish, Swedish, and English. With the leaflets, for example, we needed more copies of the Finnish version, and less than half in Swedish and English. So to save on ink and materials in general, all text was printed in black, allowing us to print all of them first, maps and images, and then adding the three different language texts last.

**How did you design the packaging to minimize materials?**

There was no packaging as such. But the size of the signage was designed to get the maximum use of a sheet of wood, while maintaining the visibility of the roadside signage.

**Which aspect of the project met the needs of CCA while having the greatest positive impacts on environmental, societal, cultural, and economic sustainability?**

The suitability of the design solution and the importance of its functionality for the end user will always take priority over purely decorative elements. While the outdoor signage didn't have a sparkly new look, its rustic feel fitted to the environment and could be used as firewood afterward in the many saunas located in the area.

**Now that the project is complete, what would you have done differently to make the project more sustainable while still meeting the client's goals?**

It would have been ideal to find a local printer to run the whole job but unfortunately due to budget and lack of suitable paper, we had the identity stationery printed in the United Kingdom and the leaflets printed in Estonia.

## Project Details

### PAPER

**Context White by Paperback Co-op**

**Specs**

100gsm

75% post-consumer waste/ 25% FSC-endorsed pulp

**Certifications**

Forest Stewardship Council (FSC)

NAPM Approved

### SIGNAGE

**Wood (after exhibition reused as firewood)**

**Certification**

Forest Stewardship Council (FSC)

### PRINTERS

**Geoff Neal Lithography**

Middlesex, UK

**Certifications, partnerships, memberships**

Forest Stewardship Council (FSC)

Carbon neutral

ISO 9001 and ISO 14001

**K-Print OÜ**

Tallinn, Estonia

**Certifications, partnerships, memberships**

Forest Stewardship Council (FSC)

Programme for the Endorsement of Forest Certification (PEFC)

The CAA book was published in late 2015. It will be an online document only, preventing further print waste and use of material.

## What advice do you have for designers just starting to integrate systems thinking into their client work?

Be clear about your goals and reasons. Find out what really matters to the client (not just what they have requested in the brief). Let these things influence you and your thought process in realizing the final outcome. Don't get too stuck on thinking design has to take a certain shape or form because it is exhibition design, information design, or anything else you would typically create.

# THE CANARY PROJECT: A MULTI-USE BOOK

**PROJECT CREDITS**

**The Canary Project**
New York, NY
www.canary-project.org

**Designers**
Edward Morris and
Dmitri Siegel

**CLIENT**

**Metropolis Books**
New York, NY
www.metropolisbooks.com

## About The Canary Project

The Canary Project is an art, design, and media studio dedicated to deepening the understanding of ecology. Originally founded in 2006 as a project to photograph landscapes throughout the world where scientists are studying the impacts of climate change, we have since supported diverse projects involving more than 100 artists, designers, writers, educators, and scientists.

Our focus is on cultivating research-intensive projects that contribute to knowledge building and are able to communicate that knowledge in a way that both respects complexity and inspires respect for life.

## What is this project about and what were the project goals?

Green Patriot Posters (Figure 4.17 through 4.22) is a multi-channel campaign centered on posters that encourage all US citizens to take part in building a sustainable economy. It was started in 2008 and is still ongoing. Our goal is to invigorate the sustainability movement with images of strength, urgency, optimism, and unity. We want the movement to connect with culture in a way that moves beyond clichés. To this end, we have commissioned posters from design leaders and developed an online community for sharing and voting on original designs. We have collected more than 800 designs to date and are constantly receiving new ones. It is our mission to distribute these designs as broadly as possible, which we have done via exhibitions, workshops, billboards, online sharing, spin-off campaigns (such as Vote the Environment) and a book (which is the topic of this case study).

We wanted to publish some of the posters we amassed in the course of The Green Patriot Posters project and to expand the reach of the project. The goal was to disseminate the message as widely as possible and to energize commitment to the sustainability movement. The publisher, Metropolis Books, shared this goal in every way. Metropolis Books is an amazing publisher that aims to "publish books that matter" and cites sustainability and the environment among its core interests. Of course, the publisher also needed to make money with the book (lest it

Figure 4.17 Green Patriot Posters book cover. (Adapted from Shepard Fairey, Global Warming, 2009, Shepard Fairey/ ObeyGiant.com.)

Figure 4.18 Essay by Steven Heller.

Figure 4.19 Nick Dewar, Simplicity is the Key to Successful Living, 2009.

Figure 4.20 Will Etling, Sustain, 2010.

Figure 4.21 Green Patriot Poster book cover (back). (Design by Dmitri Siegel and Edward Morris.)

Figure 4.22 Poster in Action: Jason Hardy, Bike Your City, 2010.

go out of business and become unable to publish any books that matter). Profit became a conflict when we raised the idea of using sustainable parameters to print the book.

### How did you guide Metropolis Books to the best possible solution to improve the triple bottom line?

Deciding to print sustainably to the extent we wanted was a big problem, particularly two weeks before press. We decided it was not enough to simply use FSC-certified paper and print it in China. Our goal was to print domestically (to save on transportation emissions); we wanted to use renewable energy credits, etc. Further, we came up with the idea that the posters in the book should be detachable so that the book could actually be useful. Diana Murphy, co-publisher of Metropolis Books, was very receptive to the idea of printing sustainability but also understood the additional cost for doing it that way (particularly using a domestic printer rather than printing in China) was either going to completely destroy margins or make the book very expensive, thereby sabotaging our goal of reaching as many people as possible. We could not make a costly book that we were encouraging people to rip apart to use the individual pages as actual posters. So Diana agreed that we would have to do the project with integrity or to kill it. That meant we would have to find donor money or some sort of subvention. And, we had two weeks to do it.

### What challenges did you encounter when trying to design the project in the most sustainable way possible? How did you overcome those challenges?

The real challenge was cost, but that was a huge challenge. Initially, I had no idea what "sustainable printing" really meant. For this, Eric Benson, who was one of the designers included in the "Green Patriot Posters" book, and Re-nourish were of invaluable help. We literally would have had no idea as to what to do without this resource. To face the cost challenge, our first task was to figure out bottom line how much more it would cost to do it the right way. We got quotes from maybe five or six printers. Most were out of the ballpark expensive—about double or even triple the cost of printing in China. Finally, Monroe Litho gave us a great quote, which was still quite a bit higher than we needed. Now we just had to find really generous, like-minded funding partners who could save the project in two weeks! I want to point out that funders can be true collaborators and that is certainly true in this case. They are: the Environmental Defense Fund, Richard H. Goodwin, Judith Bell, Neva Goodwin, Gabe Nugent, Hiscock & Barclay, and one anonymous donor. My good friend Clay Rockefeller was also invaluable in spearheading the drive to find donors, as was my creative partner Dmitri Siegel.

### How did The Canary Project design the book to use minimal materials?

The books were produced on a Heidelberg CD102 Offset Sheetfed Press (maximum sheet 28″ × 40″). The size of the book was determined based on the 28″ × 40″ sheet size to minimize waste, improve efficiencies in production, and

## Project Details

### COVER PAPER

**Mohawk Loop Antique Vellum Cover**

Specs

18pt cover

80% post-consumer waste

### INTERIOR PAPER

**Mohawk ViaPC100 Text**

Specs

18pt cover

100% post-consumer waste

Certifications

Forest Stewardship Council (FSC)

Green Seal

Green-e

Processed chlorine-free (PCF)

### INK

Specs

Vegetable-based

### PRINTER

**Monroe Litho**
Rochester, NY

Certifications, partnerships, memberships

Forest Stewardship Council (FSC)

Sustainable Green Printing Partnership (SGP)

EPA Green Power Partner

Certified Green Business

maximize the printable area—97% of the paper was used, resulting in only 3% waste.

## Which aspect of the project met Metropolis Books' needs while having the greatest positive impact on the triple bottom line?

On the positive side: we not only did print the book sustainably (100% wind power, 100% PCW fiber, soy inks, printed domestically) but also designed the back of the book into a poster titled "Print & Design Responsibly!" that contained data on the environmental benefits of printing the book the way we did (258 trees preserved for the future; 744 lbs of waterborne waste not created, etc.). I think in many ways this back cover was the best part of the book. Even by simply picking up the book, people saw the message. A total of 10,000 copies of the book were printed, and it went on to be featured in many leading museums such as the Walker Arts Center, the Cooper Hewitt Smithsonian Museum, etc. The book greatly increased the visibility of the project and spread an important message. It would have lacked integrity and failed essentially without the sustainable printing.

On the negative side: the reliance on donors presents an obvious problem—it can be nearly impossible to raise money, and it is not economically sustainable. Further, we tried to leverage our commitment to printing sustainably in order to get other authors to make the same commitment. Unfortunately, we did not manage to convince other authors to follow our lead.

Now that the project is complete, what would you have done differently to make the project more sustainable while still meeting Metropolis Books' goals?

I am not aware that there is anything more that we could have done to print the book sustainably. There were probably more that could have been done on the distribution side like not using shrink wrap or more emission-efficient shipping. However, we did not have control over these decisions unless we published a print-on-demand book, which would not have had the same cultural impact. It's likely we could not have the detachable pages with print-on-demand publishing. The donor-dependent model was problematic in that it was not economically scalable or sustainable. That's a big problem. It would be great to have publishers sign some sort of commitment letter and hold that out as a badge of honor. Who can lead the charge on this?

What advice do you have for designers just starting to integrate systems thinking into their client work?

Voice your passion! People really respond to emotional dedication. Obviously, you don't want to hurt your business by being imperious, but you can be passionate without pleading or being heavy handed. Explain why the values of sustainable printing align with the values of the client. Explain why ecology is the future in a positive way!!

# DESIGNING CULTURES STUDIO: REVERSIBLE AND RECYCLABLE PACKAGING

## PROJECT CREDITS

**Designing Cultures Studio**

Singapore
www.designingculturesstudio.com

**Designers**

Jesvin Yeo and Alving Ng

**Copywriter**

Clarence Toh

## CLIENT

**Jay Cee Global Pte Ltd**

Singapore
www.botanicascent.com

## About Designing Cultures Studio

The Designing Cultures Studio is an award-winning studio specializing in visual communication, branding communication, spatial design, and environmental graphics in the commercial and cultural fields.

Founded in 2008 by Jesvin Yeo, the studio has championed a range of design projects through the exploration of Singapore history, language, politics, everyday objects, as well as collaboration with international artists and traditional craftsmen.

The Designing Cultures Studio has been commissioned by government organizations and international brands, such as National Heritage Board, Singapore;

Tourism Board, Singapore; The Ministry of Education, The Ministry of Community Development, Youth and Sports, Singapore; Chinatown Business Association, Singapore; Santa Barbara Polo & Racquet Club; Botanicascent; and The Brand Union. Among other international design awards, the studio received are the Red Dot Award (Communication Design), A' Design Award, Good Design Award, and iF Communication Design Award.

## What were the project goals?

Organic products are usually viewed as expensive goods affordable only by the wealthy. Working to change that misconception, Botanicascent, a new skin and hair care brand by Jay Cee Global, aims to provide affordable and truly natural body care products. Working closely with small-scale local soapmakers to promote sustainable living within the community, every bar of Botanicascent soap is handmade by these soapmakers to ensure that each of the soap bars is made passionately and infused with real ingredients that are safe for all living things while raising awareness of the many benefits of using responsibly wild-crafted, natural, and organically grown botanicals. Seeing that traditional or hand-crafted production has given way to machinery and factories, this project also seeks to preserve the olive oil production of handmade soap technology by creating business opportunities for these local soapmakers.

Made and designed in Singapore, I was tasked to create a cost-effective, unique, and eye-catching packaging design that stands out from other Singaporean competitors. The target audiences were young executives who use only the finest ingredients.

## Were the sustainable parameters for this project introduced by Jay Cee Global, Designing Cultures Studio, or both?

The client inspired the sustainable parameters for this project. Before the start of the project, the client brought the design team and myself to visit the local soapmakers and to understand the production process of the products. Motivated by the natural and organically grown botanicals used, we decided to design the packaging with sustainable materials.

## How did you guide Jay Cee Global to the best possible solution to improve the triple bottom line?

As part of our effort to conserve the environment, instead of designing individual packages for each type of soap bar, we designed a single package that can be used for every soap bar within the Botanicascent brand. The client appreciated the idea immediately, as it matched their mission to be eco-friendly and also cost effective.

We first studied and narrowed down soap bar products into two themes: organic and natural. Then we designed a reversible package that can be used for both types of soap bar. Using only folding, no glue, and one color printing, the beauty of the packaging lies in how a flat piece of material can turn into a floral illustration natural soap box with rolling movement and interlock. It is also reversible to form a solid-colored packaging for the organic soap bar (Figures 4.23–4.26).

In the area of social responsibility and economics, by using only one-color printing, we were able to give the project to a small-scale local printer who owned only two-color printing machines.

## What challenges did you encounter when trying to design the packaging in the most sustainable way possible? How did you overcome those challenges?

The one-color printing was the main challenge during the design process. Typically, packaging design of skin and hair care products is vibrant and uses four-color images. Therefore, when we proposed to use one-color and sans-serif fonts for the design, it raised a lot of questions as to what was suitable for women's skin and hair care products. After a few rounds of discussions, we finally came to a solution of adding floral illustrations to give the packaging a softer feel. The client was happy after this change and accepted the design after seeing the mock-ups.

## How did you design the packaging to minimize materials?

The design of the packaging minimized resources as it was a single design that can be used for every soap bar within the Botanicascent brand, whether it be green tea, lemongrass, or goat milk. The one-color printing solution also helped to cut back on ink usage.

Figure 4.23 Botanicascent Reversible Packaging Design. (Using a rolling movement and interlock, the design can be formed into a floral illustration and also a solid-colored package.)

Figure 4.24 Botanicascent Reversible Packaging Design—floral Illustration.

Figure 4.25 Botanicascent Reversible Packaging Design—solid color.

Figure 4.26 Botanicascent Packaging Design with handmade soap.

## Which aspect of the project met Jay Cee Global's needs while having the greatest positive impacts on environmental, societal, cultural, and economic sustainability?

We felt that the aspects that met the client's needs and still had positive impacts on environmental, societal, cultural, and economic sustainability were: first, the packaging design met market criteria of performance and cost—it is easy to use and affordable; second, it enhanced the use of recycled materials—the 100%

## Project Details

PAPER

**Cyclus Print**

Specs
250gsm
Coated
100% post-consumer waste

Certifications
Forest Stewardship Council (FSC)
NAPM approved 100% recycled
EcoLabel
ISO 14001
Blue Angel
Processed chlorine-free (PCF)

PRINTER

**Kelvin Printing Pte. Ltd**
Singapore

recycled materials were safe and healthy for individuals and communities throughout their life cycle; third, the reversible design and single-color printing process helped to reduce waste and carbon footprint; and finally, through the affordable strategy, the long-term goal of this project aims to encourage more people to use only natural ingredients that are cruelty free and do not contain harsh chemicals, phthalates, harmful synthetic oils, or artificial by-products. Ultimately, we hope what we designed can help create a world that we are proud to pass onto the next generation.

Now that the project is complete, what would you have done differently to make the project more sustainable while still meeting the client's goals?

In retrospect, I would have given the packaging a "second life" after the "purchase" stage. For instance, the packaging box can turn into a soap holder, or any other form of "second life" that can be extended from the packaging.

What advice do you have for designers just starting to integrate systems thinking into their client work?

My advice to young designers would be to try not to design packaging that needs to be created specifically for a client's product, for example, the need to cast a mold to form the packaging. Instead, study all the existing materials, be creative, and come up with the best design solutions that meet your client's need, yet improve the triple bottom line.

If possible, try your best to use materials that are made from raw ingredients that grow quickly, like bamboo. Bamboo is better than a normal tree because it only needs three years to reach its full height compared with a tree which needs more than ten years. Bamboo also requires no harmful agricultural chemicals to thrive. Bamboo fiber is also stronger and lighter than tree fiber, requiring less additives and brighteners to produce.

**Backyard Creative**
Nanaimo, BC, Canada
www.backyardcreative.ca

**Project Management**
Lisa Hemingway

**Lead Designer and Art Direction**
Lisa Hemingway

**Brand Mythology**
Megan Sheldon

**Production Designer**
Grace Cheng

**Photographers**
Landon Sveinson, Lindsay Janes

**Website Development**
Melanie Karlik

Copywriters
Leif Bogwald, Jenn Bogwald

Copy Editor
Mike Muir

**Vancouver Island Expeditions
Ltd (VIE)**
Nanaimo, BC, Canada
www.VancouverIslandExpeditions.com

## About Backyard Creative

Backyard Creative is a small graphic design shop operating on the inherent belief that high-quality design can effect positive change in our communities. Lisa Hemingway, the proprietor, is a collaborative creative strategist and graphic designer living and working in BC. Lisa believes good design not only communicates efficiently and embodies the craft of design but also considers its environmental, social, and economic impacts.

## Describe the VIE project

Vancouver Island Expeditions (VIE), a start-up eco-tourism company, enlisted the help of Backyard Creative to bring their vision to life with strength and authenticity. In collaboration with Megan Sheldon of Narrative Communications, we set out to define what their core values were and to capture a brand narrative that would see them through the start-up years and exude confidence in partners and guests alike. This definition process helped to solidify the company's goals, audience, and positioning leading up to its launch.

Building on the work completed in the discovery phase and the brand narrative, we created a visual brand to communicate their company values and service, targeting an international clientele of primarily European travelers. We worked with local photographers, printers, and web developers because, like Backyard Creative, VIE believes in supporting local business. We produced user-friendly brand assets, templates, and print collateral before creating a flexible website that will continue to grow with the company.

## What were the project goals? What did VIE want the end result to achieve?

The primary objective was to clarify VIE's values and create a professional, trustworthy brand that both customers and partners could rely on. We discussed how a strong brand platform is essential in launching a business as you don't often get a second chance to make a first impression. As VIE was a start-up, we worked with them closely to clarify their company's values by going through Megan Sheldon's in-depth "Brand Narrative" process before setting out to create a visual identity.

The secondary objective was to get people excited about curated small group travel and to build awareness of VIE's new brand. VIE's tours are the best way to see Vancouver Island, and their approach is unique. Without a strong visual presence for local competitors, the goal was to make VIE stand out as professional to their international and local audiences.

Another goal was to print all materials locally to support Vancouver Island businesses. As VIE services the tourism industry on Vancouver Island by creating partnerships with existing vendors (i.e., kayak companies, tourist attractions, B&Bs, etc.), it was important to our client that their promotions be done using local businesses to be consistent with their values.

### Were the sustainable parameters for this project introduced by the VIE, Backyard Creative, or both?

VIE was attracted by Backyard Creative's portfolio of work and values. We believe in supporting local business, reducing environmental impact, and educating. It was a mutual agreement to work with sustainability in mind which definitely made for much more productive meetings and decisions along the way.

### How did you guide VIE to the best possible solution to improve the triple bottom line?

To start with, we discussed the desired marketing channels, costs, and target audience with our client at length before deciding a rack card would be the best use of their funds. We agreed that a multi-page document could become out of date quickly and seem wasteful to users, whereas a rack card would not need to be reprinted annually. As a result of these decisions, we were able to save money on printing, which enabled us to use 100% recycled paper, print a larger run, and use local photography.

We convinced the client not to purchase stock photography because we needed authentic, location-specific images to communicate their brand values. The goal was to support local photographers; however, a photo shoot was not possible due to the fact that this project timeline occurred during the tourism off-season. A few island photographers had collections of images they were willing to license to VIE. Even though this was more costly than purchasing stock photography, we were able to keep money in the local economy.

### What challenges did you encounter when trying to design the project in the most sustainable way possible? How did you overcome those challenges?

The local printer was not FSC certified but we were able to print the business cards (Figure 4.27 through 4.34) on our preferred paper stock (100% PCW). However, this printer was unable to print the rack cards locally, so we hired a different company for this. The trade-off in this situation was paper choice. In order to print the rack cards locally and to keep the project affordable, we chose the printer's in-house paper stock. Managing a project with two different printers was a bit challenging. In the end, VIE felt it was more important to be able to support local businesses.

As is often the challenge with small businesses, we didn't have a huge budget to work with. Our approach is always to prioritize client needs and work backward from the budget. It was certainly hard to manage the scope of this project but regular check-ins and clearly outlined deliverables in our agreement kept us on track. It's always beneficial to have some flexibility in your agreement to be able to tackle little shifts in priorities as the project goes forward. On the contrary, it is also important to know what to constrain in order to keep the budget manageable for you and the client (who wants to pay you well!).

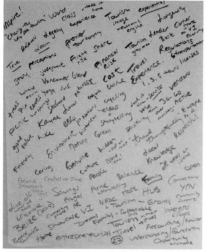

**Figure 4.27** Story Tree.

**Figure 4.28** Brand Narrative.

**Figure 4.29** Sketches.

Figure 4.30 Logo and variations.

Figure 4.31 Website. (Website wordpress theme was "Crux" created by CodeStag http://demo.codestag.com/?theme=crux and customized for VIE by developer Melanie Karlik.)

## How did Backyard Creative create this project to use minimal materials?

Instead of a large brochure outlining all the tours, we designed a single rack card that would encourage potential clients to visit our website. On the backside, we made a checklist of all the experiences that one should have on Vancouver Island to reinforce the company's core values. This decision was made to show potential VIE clients that this is a different, more thoughtful tour company which was focused on providing unique client experience, not just standard, in the most popular destinations.

Figure 4.32  Business card.

Figure 4.33  Rack card.

Figure 4.34  Tour schedule.

Which aspect of the project met VIE's needs while having the greatest positive impacts on environmental, societal, cultural, and economic sustainability?

The client has received a lot of positive feedback about their brand image since officially launching in May 2014. Leif Bogwald, VIE owner and travel curator, remarked, "I've definitely had great feedback on the brand and people have contacted me based on what I think is a very professional look."

The positive impacts, although difficult to measure, begin with VIE's mission and purpose: "We create authentic, intimate and memorable visitor experiences while honoring the culture, heritage, and natural beauty of Vancouver Island. Discover places that inspire stories." The client's ethos to respect nature with low-impact tours and leave-no-trace hiking are promoted to all travelers. Working with local businesses and promoting other small businesses to help the tourism industry on Vancouver Island thrive have a positive impact on the local economy and residents. VIE promotes local traditions, customs, and "island" lifestyle by helping people take a pause and truly understand the culture on the island. Investing in VIE's brand early on will contribute to the ongoing success of the company and will also result in the success of VIE's collaborators.

Now that the project is complete, what would you have done differently to make the project more sustainable while still meeting VIE's goals?

Although we're very happy with what we were able to accomplish with a modest budget, we would have liked to spend a little more time polishing the website. Some of the pages need refinements on mobile and the Wordpress template; although well designed, they did have their limitations when it came to customization.

Although we were considerate of a European clientele, and installed a Google Translate plug-in, we would have also liked the chance to work directly with translators to ensure that the site communicated properly in other languages. We see this website as beta version 1.0 and look forward to refining it in the future with VIE.

To help garner excitement about small group travel, we proposed the creation of a blog and a Facebook page. As their business grows, we'd love to see more marketing by way of photos and stories on their website!

What advice do you have for designers just starting to integrate systems thinking into their client work?

Think about what the goals are for the project and question all constraints from the very beginning of the project. For example, when our client said, "We need a brochure outlining all of our tours," we replied, "you need to communicate the variety of the tours that you offer to get the largest number of potential customers to your website." By approaching the problem from the perspective of their

## Project Details

**Mohawk Options i-Tone Inxwell**

Specs
130# Cover
100% post-consumer waste

Certifications
Forest Stewardship Council (FSC)
Green Seal
Green-e
Processed chlorine-free (PCF)
Carbon-neutral business

RACK CARD

**TopKote Dull Cover**

Specs
100# cover
10% post-consumer waste
Digitally printed

Certifications
Forest Stewardship Council (FSC)

PRINTERS

**Elite Image (Business Card)**
Nanaimo, BC, Canada

**Print Three (Rack Card)**
Nanaimo, BC, Canada

Certifications
Forest Stewardship Council (FSC)

HOSTING

**WebNames.ca**
Vancouver, BC, Canada
www.webnames.ca

key objectives, we eliminated the need for a multi-page print piece. Instead, we focused on featuring tours on the VIE website. The client's budget was then freed up for more essential expenditures such as defining their brand narrative at the project start to focus on subsequent work and acquire high-quality, local photography.

Also, it's important to learn what your client values and stay true to that throughout the process. For example, if the client's business focuses on connecting and promoting local businesses, be sure to work with local businesses when creating their promotional materials (i.e., use of local printers and photographers).

Finally, be sure to consider the end of the life-cycle first. It was important that the rack card extends beyond its main objective of driving people to the website or making an inquiry. For instance, our goal with the VIE rack card was to provide people with a clear and attractive visual that they might pin up at home or at work to remind them of all the great experiences to look for when traveling.

# METALLI LINDBERG: CREATING A BUZZ

## About Metalli Lindberg

Located in Conegliano Veneto near Treviso, Italy, Metalli Lindberg is a communications and design laboratory. Services include strategy, consulting, research, art direction, and publishing. The company creates advertising, design for print, identities, signage, interiors, websites, packaging, exhibitions, and events materials.

With an approach that is based both on science and art, the company's designers see the choice of an image, a graphic sign, or a font type not as an end in itself but as a means of reaching a goal and of conveying a concept in a straightforward and original way. The end result of this method for design problem solving is that "communication is visible, tangible and represents an intelligent and positive investment." All of these factors support Metalli Lindberg's goal of contributing to the world in which it resides, while disseminating values that include ethics and sustainability.

Figure 4.35 First BEE sketch.          Figure 4.36 First BEE identity.

## What were the project goals?

Conapi is one of the most important cooperatives of beekeepers in Europe and represents nearly 600 beekeepers throughout Italy. We recognized a great opportunity for Conapi to share their endless resources, knowledge, and experience to help create more awareness of the current plight of declining bees in Italy. We developed a proposal for a series of coordinated materials, instruments, and initiatives to show the client how the project could be implemented. BEE ACTIVE! highlights the plight and decline in the bee population in Italy (as it is in the rest of the world). Our goal for the project, and that of our clients, was simply to create more awareness and to help people become a little more "BEE ACTIVE!" toward understanding and helping bees (Figures 4.35 through 4.42).

## Were the sustainable parameters for this campaign introduced by Conapi, Metalli Lindberg, or both?

These were introduced by both the studio and the client, wherever possible. It was fundamental to the project that any materials produced were environmentally friendly and of a controlled quantity.

## How did you guide Conapi to the best possible solution to improve the triple bottom line?

The client is already sensitive to certain issues due to the nature of their business and a background in organic farming. It was very important that the content was easy-to-read, stimulating, and accessible to create further interest and learn more about the life of bees. There was to be no sensational, dramatic, or banal content—only constructive and helpful information that could be appreciated by people of all ages. The use of materials was also important to reflect the nature of the initiative; hence, the use of the biodegradable honey tub and Crush paper, which is made with residue from food crops and post-consumer waste fiber. The paper is also manufactured with 100% green energy from hydroelectricity and emissions offset with carbon credits.

Figure 4.37 First BEE cover.

Figure 4.38 First BEE interior spread 1.

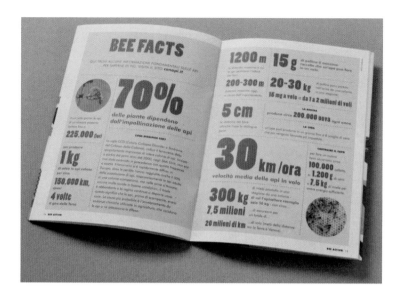

Figure 4.39  First BEE interior spread 2.

Figure 4.40  First BEE honey tubs.

Figure 4.41 First BEE pins.

Figure 4.42 First BEE cards.

## Project Details

### PAPER

**Crush by Favini**

### Specs

15% process residues from organic products (citrus fruits, corn, olives, coffee, kiwi fruits, hazelnuts, and almonds)

30% post-consumer waste

GMO free

Made with 100% hydroelectric power

### Certifications

Forest Stewardship Council (FSC)

### PAPER CUP

**Bioplat-Bio-line**

### Specs

Pure pulp solid board combined with PLA film

### Certifications

Forest Stewardship Council (FSC)

100% biodegradable and compostable according to Standard EN 13432.

### PRINTER

**Eurostampa**
Bologna, Italy

## Which aspect of the project met Conapi's needs while having the greatest positive impacts on environmental, societal, cultural, and economic sustainability?

The project was well received by both Conapi and the public. Members of the cooperative of beekeepers were especially pleased with the extra support. The project has also been a partner in a TV/publishing campaign and is currently active in some schools.

## Now that the project is complete, what would you have done differently to make the project more sustainable while still meeting Conapi's goals?

The project still continues. We are working with Conapi on the website and on an additional print project. Offering more activity and events on the web are in the pipeline, which will make the project more accessible to a greater number of people. There are also plans for the initiative to collaborate with other partners in the food sector.

## What advice do you have for designers just starting to integrate systems thinking into their client work?

Integrating good systems thinking improves any project by making it more effective, richer in content, and more accessible to its audience. Systems thinking encourages creativity and can enhance project longevity, thereby creating communication that's beneficial both to the client and/or the public.

- Try to look at a project as openly as possible. Be curious. Research and brainstorm to assess what can be brought to the project within and beyond the requirements of the brief. Designers should be able to reference from as many sources of information as possible to enhance any design solution such as manufacturing, new methods and processes, visual techniques, specialist suppliers, sustainable materials and disposal, etc.

- Map everything out with diagrams or infographics to present and accompany the client through the creative process. It's often here that new ideas and opportunities arise.

- In addition to the brief, come up with an idea that can inform the client and engage the public on other issues to influence further awareness. For example, add information to the project regarding ethics, sustainability or social responsibility, social concerns or lifestyle choices that can encourage behavioral change that have social value.

- Consider also both the environmental and social impact of production choices. Minimize use of materials and printing and assess the effects of distribution and mailing.

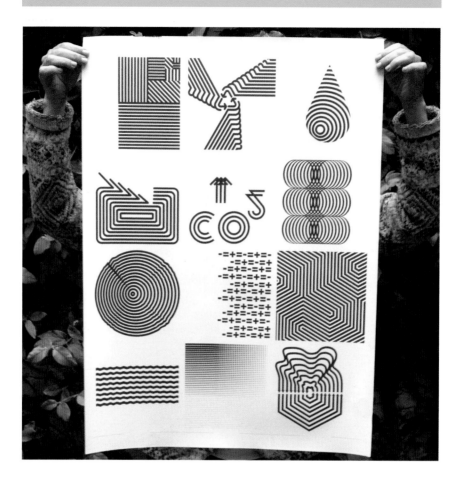

**PROJECT CREDITS**

**La PAGE Original**
Barcelona, Spain
www.lapageoriginal.com

**Creative Director**
Josep Martínez Ruzafa

**Art Director**
Sònia Martínez Ruzafa

**Designers**
Josep and Sònia Martínez Ruzafa

**Copywriter**
La PAGE Studio

**CLIENT**

**EmanaGreen**
Barcelona, Spain
www.emanagreen.com

## About La PAGE Original

La PAGE Original is a graphic design and visual communication studio that was created in 1991. The company, composed of three people, implemented and managed EMAS registration (Eco-Management and Audit Scheme) in 2011. They incorporate environmental criteria in their projects as an opportunity to improve their professional skills and apply their potential as communicators to positively influence behavioral change toward a more sustainable society.

## What were the project goals?

We wanted to demonstrate the advantages of using stone paper in a calendar (Figure 4.43 through 4.48). The main audience of this project was the potential clients who were already aware of environmental issues. However, we thought designers were an important target audience as well since we have the power to make better environmental choices during the development of a project. We felt that by making the calendar out of stone paper, we could prove its ecological worth through the design and manufacturing processes. Also, we were hoping to show the power and the responsibility we have as designers to choose better materials, processes, and coherent messaging—this was the idea behind this project. We have to be clear and re-think the way we go forward with our projects.

**Figure 4.43** Cover of stone paper calendar.

**Figure 4.44** Environmental message for June 0,0 0,0: water. The stone paper needs 0 liters of water for its fabrication.

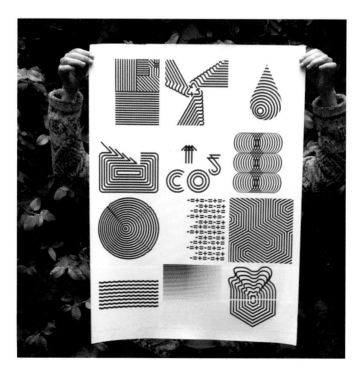

**Figure 4.45** Press sheet of the 12 pages of the calendar.

Another objective of this project was to educate people about stone paper as a more sustainable alternative in the printing industry. We wanted to promote its environmental advantages focusing on communicating to designers, printers, and other eco-friendly clients. The design of this table calendar was crafted with eco-friendly criteria and we also incorporated green messaging on every month related to sustainable design criteria.

Figure 4.46 Printout showing the transparency of the stone paper.

How did you guide EmanaGreen to the best possible solution to improve the triple bottom line?

EmanaGreen was looking at making a calendar that only communicated the advantages of using stone paper, but we felt it would be a better approach if the calendar itself were printed on stone paper. We offered this option to the client and through more discussion with the EmanaGreen team, we agreed that this was a better way to carry out the project.

Figure 4.47 Calendar page in action.

This was an eco-friendly project since the beginning (designed in a studio with a certified environmental management system—EMAS, and zero $CO_2$ emissions) with a product (stone paper) that releases 50% less carbon dioxide than paper made from tree fiber. The paper also didn't require water or toxic chemicals during its manufacture. We also worked with minimal materials and followed the same logic with inks. A big challenge was to print the whole calendar in a single printing, double-sided, with black ink. We made sure that the production was carried out by a press supported by our local government for environmental and sustainability issues. Since we used a small amount of resources, we managed to create a very economical product with strong social and environmental values.

Figure 4.48 Stone paper decomposes after a year in the sun and outdoors. The result is calcium carbonate.

## What challenges did you encounter when trying to design the calendar in the most sustainable way possible? How did you overcome those challenges?

We have developed a system to measure the environmental impact of our projects based on a life-cycle analysis. We incorporate, in our methodology, criteria to design in a more sustainable way and are able to confront new challenges.

We always want to be able to give to our clients a budget that adjusts to their needs and find suppliers and producers who guarantee their social and environmental commitments. That is one challenge we had to overcome. In this case, the characteristics of the paper required the printing process to be slower than usual (for an offset printer) and the attention during the process to be thorough. This meant we had to rely on the pressman to work out of his ordinary routine and to make this situation an opportunity to prove his commitment as a professional.

## How did you design the packaging to minimize materials?

The calendar's format takes maximum advantage of the stone paper and reduces waste. (The thickness of the stone paper was the thinner option from the manufacturer—100 microns.) Using the minimum amount of material created the effect of transparency that allowed us to play graphically with the back impressions of each leaf. The front and back pages are made from the same stone paper material, and the binding element is a spiral of aluminum that is 100% recyclable and allows disassembly in an easy way. The graphics were made without using bleeds in order to minimize ink usage.

## Project Details

### PAPER

**FiberStone® Natural Stone Paper**

### Certifications

Cradle to Cradle (Silver)

### INK

**Specs**

Vegetable (water based)

### PRINTER

**Grafiques Ortells SL**

Barcelona, Spain

### Certifications

Forest Stewardship Council (FSC)

EU Eco-Management and Audit Scheme (EMAS)

ISO 14001

## Which aspect of the project met EmanaGreen's needs while having the greatest positive impacts on environmental, societal, cultural, and economic sustainability?

The project was a great success. We got to accompany the consumers throughout the whole year. They used the stone paper, wrote in it, and understood day-by-day its qualities. We also had the opportunity to teach in a simple and direct way not only the advantages of stone paper but also how to reduce the environmental impact through better design decisions. We thought it was important to wake up the consciences of consumers with regard to environmental matters. In fact, many asked for a second edition for the following year.

## Now that the project is complete, what would you have done differently to make the project more sustainable while still meeting the client's goals?

Although the disassembly process for recycling the aluminum spiral and the paper leaves is very simple, we thought it would be interesting to be able to achieve a mono-material design so that the whole calendar could be recycled at once.

## What advice do you have for designers just starting to integrate systems thinking into their client work?

Design is a powerful profession. As the messages, objects, and experiences that we create go through hands, minds, and hearts, we have a chance to promote and achieve sustainability. We can build up a wider sense of sustainable culture through our work and suggest changes in lifestyles toward a more eco-friendly way of living. We hope that innovative concepts such as reducing resources and waste, life-cycle analysis, and sustainability become more of a part of the graphic design world. There are clearly important questions that need to be asked about the consequences of our choices when we design. We need to ask about the origin of the materials we use, who produces them, and what will happen when we no longer use them. The responsibility of our actions goes beyond only creative decision-making. We have to acknowledge our capacity to negatively impact the planet and also positively through our decisions. We have, therefore, to be respectful to the world around us.

# ECOCREATIVE: COMMUNITY-OWNED DESIGN

## PROJECT CREDITS

**Ecocreative**

Adelaide, South Australia

www.ecocreative.com.au

**Creative Director and Copywriter**
Matthew Wright-Simon

**Designers**
Robin Green

## CLIENT

**District Council of Mount Barker**

South Australia

www.dcmtbarker.sa.gov.au

## About Ecocreative

Ecocreative is a multi-faceted creative consultancy for people and planet. We specialize in strategy, design, and communications aimed at engaging the community. To establish the best opportunity for successful outcomes, Ecocreative works closely with leaders and decision-makers to better align action with organizational values.

Equal parts sustainable design studio, strategic advisory service, communications consultancy, engagement facilitator, problem solver, and think tank, Ecocreative operates as a change agent. Ecocreative's depth of experience, knowledge, and impressive networks help organizations in the government, business, and community sectors navigate, communicate, and innovate with confidence.

Ecocreative is one of Australia's founding certified B Corps.

## What were the project goals?

In establishing a community open space featuring a wetland and walking trails, our local government client wanted to ensure members of the public would "watch this space" while land redevelopment took place.

Following site visits, research, and lots of conversation, we convinced our client to consider something that would celebrate local heritage and the materiality of railway transport in its design and storytelling approach.

## Were the sustainable parameters for this project introduced by the District Council of Mount Barker, Ecocreative, or both?

As we were working with people outside of the client organization's sustainability division, engaging Ecocreative is where the client's sustainability considerations began for this project. Decisions regarding materials and processes were driven by our studio, with a particular focus on sourcing local materials and talent.

## How did you guide the District Council of Mount Barker to the best possible solution to improve the triple bottom line?

Investigation into local social issues identified that high levels of unemployment was thought to be connected to vandalism of public property. Without having the opportunity to research in depth, we had a hunch that poorly designed public places might also be having an influence. We therefore determined that anything we designed would need to be the centerpiece of a new public design approach, look impressive, and be very robust in construction. It also had to look and be so "local" that it would be owned by the community. The creation of a laser-cut steel diorama helped build depth into storytelling about a township that had until this project been very hard to find.

## What challenges did you encounter when trying to design the campaign in the most sustainable way possible? How did you overcome those challenges?

Challenges abounded with the project as it was created in the midst of a site under development, ultimately standing as the first part of a phased public park. Aside from issues related to site access, planned infrastructure, and services (including electricity for lighting), our options were limited only by budget and the availability of materials. We investigated using stone, metals, and even railway sleepers from the nearby abandoned railway siding (from which we drew design inspiration)—all of which looked to be available without the need for freight. Unfortunately, once we requested access to this material, we learned that the site was considered of possible historical significance and could not be reused. Given that the possible plundering of a "heritage site" was not the ideal way to share a story of local history, we reconsidered our approach! We instead sourced stone quarried from nearby and the services of a local stonemason, secured railway timbers harvested from an Australian family-run business, and made use of structural weathering Corten steel which has very high levels of recycled content and eliminates the need for painting. We ensured lighting was energy efficient and recommend this be linked to light sensors and solar panels (slated for installation on a yet-to-be built toilet block).

## How did you design all your pieces for the campaign to minimize materials?

Unlike much of our work, this piece needed to be imposing and to have real substance in the landscape. While we wanted to ensure the diorama was big, we still ensured the dimensions took into account the standard sizings of our defining materials—steel sheets and railway timbers, in particular. We used the full length of timbers, trimming down from this where necessary and eliminating offcuts, making full use of the timber profile. Knowing that the structural steel came in 2,400 mm × 1,200 mm sheets, we worked our design so as to make the maximum possible use of the sheet, with minimal offcuts. The selection of a structural weight meant we had no need to have additional supports in place and we minimized weld points. The diorama, timber uprights, and backing panel were partially prefabricated, and we then walled the structure in place with the help of the stonemason, using only the stone and concrete required. Our use of a durable automotive grade paint ensured strong color-fastness of the red backing panel, even though its west-facing aspect rendered it more vulnerable to UV fading (Figures 4.49 through 4.54).

## Which aspect of the project met the District Council of Mount Barker's needs while having the greatest positive impacts on environmental, societal, cultural, and economic sustainability?

The Byethorne Park diorama has been a great success, having stood for several years at the entrance to a now-popular public park, requiring no maintenance to date. We see that the flourishing heritage of the surrounding Nairne township and the connectivity of the community through urban design is in strong alignment with the optimistic approach we took to this work, given that so little was established, shared, or built beforehand. Our storytelling and design approach considered many of the strongest facets of Nairne's environmental, economic, and cultural heritage, and we see that balance is being returned to the community.

Figure 4.49 Initial concept sketch.

Figure 4.50 More developed concept sketch.

Figure 4.51 Completed structure in situ, oblique view.

Figure 4.52 Front-on view of structure.

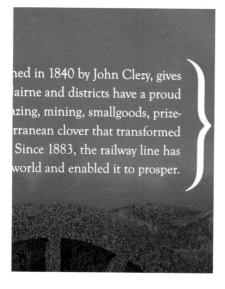

Figure 4.53 Details of historical story.

Figure 4.54 Diorama detail.

## Project Details

### MATERIALS

Corten steel sheets (10 mm thick), LED lights, housings and wiring, railway timbers, quarried stone with mortar, steel sheeting with enamel paint and vinyl stickers, fixings, and concrete footings.

### PRINTER/MANUFACTURER/ SCREEN PRINTER, ETC.

**Signscope**
Adelaide, South Australia

## Now that the project is complete, what would you have done differently to make the project more sustainable while still meeting the client's goals?

It is always interesting to reflect on a project, especially when so little is set out in the form of a brief, timetable, or budget. With the benefit of more time, we believe we would have been able to research opportunities to obtain local stone and timber to reuse, including the help of a local sawmill. We would also have been able to ensure link-ins with solar photovoltaics and battery storage, possibly enabling the feature to exist off-grid. A life-cycle analysis of the materials and processes would also have been helpful, especially given that what we delivered is something designed to last for decades with minimal maintenance.

## What advice do you have for designers just starting to integrate systems thinking into their client work?

Our advice for designers who want to consider systems thinking is to ask as many questions as possible of clients and their stakeholders about *why* something needs to be created. Learn about the objective and how this project will affect positive change in a social and cultural context.

## PROJECT CREDITS

**Cast Iron Design**
Boulder, CO
www.castirondesign.com

**Designers**
Jonathan Black and
Richard Roche

**Copywriter**
Richard Roche

### CLIENT

**Huckle & Goose**
New York, NY
www.hucklegoose.com

## About Cast Iron Design

Cast Iron Design is an environmentally responsible design studio based in Boulder, Colorado. Its mission is to pair good design with positive impact by creating memorable brands, implementing environmentally responsible practices, and helping the design community do the same.

## What were the project goals?

Anyone who has ventured into the world of seasonal cooking using farm-fresh ingredients knows it's not an easy task. Huckle & Goose—a service centered around enabling, educating, and inspiring people to cook and eat consciously—commissioned us to create an interactive web app that helps people plan and prepare meals with a focus on local foods and seasonal cooking. The goal of the project was to change behavior by creating a digital tool to make the meal planning process easier and thereby less intimidating.

Huckle & Goose approached us in part due to our commitment to environmental responsibility. They were very supportive of the sustainable solutions that we proposed—a dream client for a green graphic designer.

The key to a good client/designer relationship is trust. Once we built that trust—fostered by honesty, kindness, thoroughness, and by genuinely caring about the client's goals and mission—the rest was easy. Some of the sustainable solutions we proposed resulted in cost savings (e.g., designing for the press sheet) while others resulted in cost premiums (e.g., using organic cotton). The client was always able to see the benefits of environmental stewardship, both from an ethical perspective (doing the right thing) and a brand-building perspective (building trust and loyalty with their audience).

What challenges did you encounter when trying to design
the campaign in the most sustainable way possible? How
did you overcome those challenges?
Often the primary challenge for many sustainable print projects is the extra time required—time to research processes and materials, time for setting up press sheets, and everything else. For this specific project, we spent dozens of extra hours researching cotton production, woven label production, eco-binding options for journals, 100% recycled corrugated box sourcing, recyclability of various adhesive packaging tapes, and so on. We consider the time an investment into building our expertise and increasing our value to future clients.

Another challenge we faced was finding a top-tier, sustainably powered web host with a strong reputation for performance, reliability, and customer service. We instead decided to recommend the client offset their website's energy use themselves. We purchased Renewable Energy Certificates (RECs) (in this case representing energy generated via wind power) through Terrapass and indirectly offset our hosting based on the average energy used for a single server, plus 25% extra (dictated by the minimum purchase required by Terrapass). Our host, and most hosting providers in general, would not divulge information about how many sites are hosted per server, but based on our plan allowance and the typical capabilities of a server, we estimate the offsets purchased are at least four times the amount needed for our client's site (and potentially even over 25 times).

We designed each print item backward, allowing the size of the press sheet to determine the size of the print piece (designing for the press sheet). This is a beginning step, which minimizes trim waste. The journals were designed with minimum impact (recycled materials) and maximum recyclability (dry toner inks, cotton thread). The cotton thread binding is distinctive and also highly recyclable (the cotton thread becomes part of the pulp mixture when recycled).

The nature of a fabric tote encourages reuse, and the tote's construction is sturdy, which is an important aspect of longevity and therefore sustainability (Figure 4.55 through 4.62). In addition, the tote is made of 100% organic cotton, which can be composted at the end of its life.

Figure 4.55 All of the totes had the same woven label on the inside which described the sustainability credentials of the materials and manufacturing of the custom totes.

The press kit boxes were printed with a fun "reuse this corrugated container" statement on the inside of the box, which reminds the audience to reuse the box while integrating a bit of wit and charm to the piece. We also specified WAT (water-activated tape), which is best for recyclability; however, most WAT is reinforced with fiberglass strands to add strength. These fiberglass strands are unnecessary for most lightweight contents so we opted for a nonreinforced paper tape. The tape we specified uses a starch-based adhesive that is biodegradable, making the tape 100% recyclable.

Figure 4.56 Front of business card showing blind emboss.

## Which aspect of the project met Huckle & Goose's needs while having the greatest positive impacts on environmental, societal, cultural, and economic sustainability?

The most successful outcome of the project, in terms of end result and positive impact, was the tote bags. The client championed a tote that had a positive impact on environmental and social sustainability (especially when compared with conventionally produced totes) and was exceedingly pleased with the end product. Although the totes were produced in fairly small quantities, the research that went into finding the most eco-friendly solution possible made us proud of the accomplishment. As a result, the totes are an exemplary case study in sustainable design. We were able to find a tote manufacturer that sources its organic cotton from a farm in Texas. Conventional cotton is one of the most chemically dependent crops in the world, so sourcing organic cotton (typically grown overseas) was critical. The cotton was then woven in South Carolina (again, a process often exported overseas) before being cut, sewn, and printed in New Hampshire. To top things off, we were able to find a manufacturer in the United States (an exceedingly rare find for small runs) to create the custom woven labels for the inside of the bag which served to identify the product, educate the consumer about sustainability, and—equally important—provide a chuckle or two.

Figure 4.57 Journal cover and end sheet detail.

Figure 4.58 Journal interior detail.

Now that the project is complete, what would you have done differently to make the project more sustainable while still meeting the client's goals?

The die cutting process is a great eco-friendly way to create a unique visual distinction with a printed piece (since there's no ink or materials involved beyond the creation of the die itself), but we learned that it could cause a significant amount of trim waste for small items like business cards.

What advice do you have for designers just starting to integrate systems thinking into their client work?

Systems thinking involves breaking from the status quo in the way you think about design, and often it necessitates spending considerable amounts of time researching sustainability options. Sustainability research is a bit like investigative journalism. You start with a Google search, try to make sense of a material safety data sheet (MSDS), call a sales rep to find out more information, corroborate or refute that information, and continue the cycle until you have a well-rounded collection of facts. It's a necessary extension of the designer's role as a problem solver, yet the time spent upfront can be daunting. At the same time, it's an exciting pursuit that provides an

Figure 4.59 The press kit opens up to reveal a hand-addressed written envelop attached to the inside of the lid.

Figure 4.60 Inside bottom of the screen printed box.

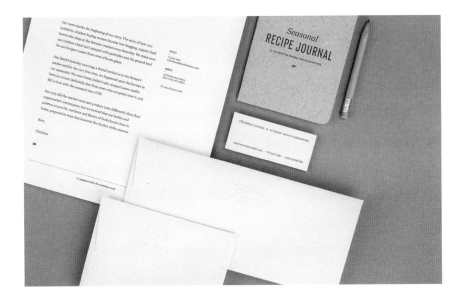

Figure 4.61 Full stationery set (business cards, letterhead, and two sizes of hand-embossed envelopes).

Figure 4.62 Kid tote.

immediate sense of accomplishment and satisfaction, and in the long term can add considerable value to your design practice.

Furthermore, some other good advice we learned is that when beginning a print project, we always include production oversight into our estimates. This is a key component of green design that is commonly overlooked.

## Project Details

### PAPER

**Mohawk Loop**

### Journal Cover Specs
Antique Vellum

80# Cover

50% PCW recycled fibers, 50% virgin fibers

Letterpress printed

### Journal Interior Specs
Smooth Ivory

24# Writing

100% post-consumer waste (PCW) recycled fibers

Digitally printed with dry toner

### Business Card Specs
Antique Vellum (Milkweed)

160# Double Thick Cover

100% post-consumer waste (PCW) recycled fibers

Letterpress printed, blind embossed, and die cut

### Letterhead Specs
Smooth (Ivory)

24# Writing

100% post-consumer waste (PCW) recycled fibers

Laser printed on-demand by client to minimize waste

### Envelope Specs
Antique Vellum (Milkweed + Birch)

80# Text

100% post-consumer waste (PCW) recycled fibers

Blind embossed with hand embosser

### Mohawk Loop Certifications
Forest Stewardship Council (FSC)

Processed Chlorine Free (PCF)

Manufactured carbon neutral (RECs certified by Green-e®)

Green Seal Certified

Acid Free

### JOURNAL ENDSHEETS PAPER
**French Paper Company**

### Specs
Steel Blue

80# text

100% recycled fibers (30% post-consumer, 70% pre-consumer)

Manufactured carbon neutral (with on-site hydroelectricity)

Digitally printed with dry toner

### Certifications
Processed Chlorine Free (PCF)

### PRESS KIT MAILER
**Globe Guard Corrugated Tuck Mailer**

### Specs
100% recycled fibers (% PCW varies)

Interior protected with 100% recycled kraft tissue paper

Exterior sealed with kraft paper non-reinforced WAT (water activated tape)

Screen printed with water-based inks and nontoxic biodegradable screen reclaiming chemicals

### Certifications
Forest Stewardship Council (FSC)

Processed Chlorine Free (PCF)

**Enviro-tote Market Tote and Mini Tote**

Specs

Unbleached organic cotton grown in Texas and woven in South Carolina, USA

Cut, sewn, and screen printed using phthalate-free inks in New Hampshire, USA

Interior label made in Vermont, USA (unknown cotton blend, not organic)

JOURNAL INTERIORS & PROMO CARDS PRINTER

**Colt Printing**
Boulder, CO

BUSINESS CARDS & JOURNAL COVERS PRINTER

**Smokeproof Press**
Boulder, CO

TOTES

Enviro-tote
Bedford, NH

Certifications

Fair Labor Association, Category C license

BOXES

**Printed in the Cast Iron Design screen printing studio,**
Boulder, CO.

HOSTING

**Linode
Certifications**
W3C compliant

Renewable Energy Certificates (RECs) through Terrapass

# Chapter 5

## TODAY

The goal we set forth in the planning stages of this book was to map a sustainable path ahead for the graphic design profession. We would base this on best practices, practical insights gleaned from case studies, guidance from industry experts, and our own experience. We didn't necessarily believe that the direction forward would be presented in a neat and tidy package, but there are some smart connected approaches for a more responsible design practice we charted out for you in this chapter. Despite the impactful lessons, it seemed that for every positive best practice tip we received or piece of upbeat news we read, environmental and social progress were tempered by dire international reports on global warming impacts, oil spills, wildlife extinction, or arduous political battles between ideology and common sense. Although discouraging and sometimes hopeless, it made us realize how important designing for sustainability truly is.

We also found somewhat unsurprisingly that in our professional lives, consistently implementing sustainability best practices and our systems thinking strategies proved difficult at times. It was especially challenging when a project timeline was too aggressive or the client was not of the same mindset. We often came across clients unwilling to try new approaches fearful of the immediate cost being more important than future gains or were mired in the past—"we always do it this way, why change it?" These obstacles, however, made us ask ourselves again the very same questions that inspired us to write this book. How do we integrate systems thinking and sustainable outcomes with everyday print or digital projects? How do we effectively convince our clients or our employers the importance of sustainable design? There isn't always a bullet-proof answer that works in every scenario, but clear case studies in this book and beyond offer strategies that can help.

The underlying theme of all the case studies, however, is that to design sustainably, it's important to understand that our world is connected by a balance of interlocking biological systems—systems which should be mimicked as opposed to being destroyed through design work. These systems are sustainable where the stocks and flows are circular and replenishing. This fact clearly indicates that graphic designers must become more skilled at creating responsibly in this teeming world of complex and delicate ecosystems. This takes time. Time which must be spent exploring, trying, failing, and trying again to learn more about designing with systems and sharing this knowledge (yet another reason why we wrote this book). The path forward is one like your grandfather described to you as his childhood journey—uphill both ways and full of potholes.

## INSIGHTS FROM OUR CASE STUDIES

When we sent out the call for submissions for this book, we were optimistically looking to learn how designers persuade hesitant or resistant clients to implement triple bottom line focused projects using systems thinking. Since this process is relatively new to graphic design, we knew it would be a challenge to locate exclusively case studies that implemented systems thinking. Within the submitted case studies, we found that a few studios were mapping systems of interaction and impact internally or with their client, while a few others were actually thinking in systems whether they realized it or not. That was promising. However, all the case studies we received did not meet our second goal of achieving balanced triple bottom line results with *resistant* clients. Instead, all of the ten case studies involved a studio or designer working with like-minded clients.

Despite this, all the case studies combined provide an interesting snapshot of where graphic design is today with regard to sustainability and systems thinking. We feel as a collective that these projects' stories can help shift our role as graphic designers from strictly service providers to systems design strategists and eventually help transform the profession into one with a healthier and more sustainable future. The valuable reflections from each of the case studies illustrate how the design studio or designer proposed unique sustainable solutions to various obstacles when working with clients and vendors. When there were bumps in the road, the designers challenged the traditional, resource-intensive, and "easy" status-quo solution to achieve the most sustainable result. This section of the chapter is a general overview of all the case studies' best practices that, most importantly, are extremely practical and can be implemented today. The collection of lessons learned is also a living document that the graphic design community can continue to explore and build upon with ideas for future projects and challenges. All of the following tips are more easily implemented by designing using systems thinking. Zooming in and out of different social, environmental, and economic relationships helps designers understand the opportunities, impacts, strengths, and weaknesses of different design decisions. Beyond trying out the techniques described in the case studies, it is paramount that time and practice is invested in systems thinking. Understanding how one can design more meaningful, sustainable, and usable outcomes with biological systems as a guide will provide a means to reach the seemingly unattainable triple bottom line.

Map the project and its impacts

As described in Chapter 2, to think in systems means understanding that our world is interconnected and consequently a general knowledge of our biological systems is vital to create positive impacts. Environmental Studies Professor David Orr elaborates: "(d)esigning with nature disciplines human intentions with the growing knowledge of how the world works as a physical system. The goal is not total mastery but harmony that causes no ugliness, human or ecological, somewhere else or at some later time. And it is not just about making things, but rather remaking the human presence in the world in a way that honors life and protects human dignity."[1] Understanding the project goals and mapping the audiences, outcomes, vendors (and their geographic locations), and finally evaluating the possibilities from these will help visualize where your decisions have positive and negative effects. Modern Species found that "(o)nce you know where you can make a big impact, you can focus your design thinking on those issues to find better solutions to difficult problems." Metalli Lindberg's case study explains that mapping using diagrams or infographics often leads to unexpected or fresh ideas and that's when new business and creative opportunities can arise.

Backyard Creative's brainstorming sketches and story tree is another example of an approach to mapping. In our own experiences with mapping, we've used pretty much anything handy from the ubiquitous Post-It notes to white boards or the backs of used napkins from the local coffee shop. (Generally, we've found that mapping out the project by hand has proven much more effective for team collaboration and rapid visualization.) Reviewing this map or, even better, creating one with the client is a more convincing method to ensure a solutions approach to a balanced triple bottom line and also serves as a guide to navigate the designer and the client through the creative process.

The argument against using systems thinking suggests if you are always trying to focus on the entire system, then you will never be able to focus on any one thing, and you may never find solutions to anything. We disagree. It's like saying,

"If it's too difficult, don't try." So the suggestion of working with the client is an important one as creating a map as a team or simultaneously with the users allows more eyes on the prize of positive impact. As working in groups sometimes necessitates, the creation of the map can also be broken into more manageable chunks assigned to smaller teams tasked to focus exclusively on people, planet, or profit, or instead to delegate duties to gather data or explore alternative materials and ideas. Whichever way you complete this map of the project, be aware that designers are not experts in everything and sharing it with your team or client will be most beneficial and effective. Freelancers, usually working solo, may face some additional challenges with systems thinking, where group discussion is important. We suggest again that creating a map with the client will help, but remember there is always a large network of peers that can be available for brainstorming over a Fair Trade cup of Joe.

## Work locally and choose renewables

Backyard Creative and their client, Vancouver Island Expeditions, made working with local vendors a priority. Compared with large chain stores, locally owned businesses reinvest a much larger amount of their revenue back into the local economy. This is called the *Local Multiplier Effect*. On average, for every one dollar spent at a local business, about half of that dollar, 48% to be exact,[2] is reinvested in local area, while, in comparison, a chain store only reinvests roughly 15 cents of that same dollar back into the community.[3] Many studies have also shown that median income has risen faster in communities with more thriving local businesses, as larger international box stores can depress wages and benefits and decrease the number of retail jobs in the area.[4] Dr. Stephen J. Goetz from Penn State University proved (in both rural and urban settings) communities with "larger density of small, locally owned businesses experienced greater per capita income growth between 2000 and 2007."[5]

The positive effects of doing business locally do not end there (Figure 5.1). Supporting local businesses also helps develop a better sense of community by strengthening social and economic relationships which in turn can lead to happier people and greater resident retention. In fact, a 2011 study found that "(c)ounties with a vibrant small-business sector have lower rates of mortality and a lower prevalence of obesity and diabetes."[6] Walkable downtowns, greater community

48¢

15¢

Local    Chain

Figure 5.1 For every one dollar spent at a local business, about 48 cents is rein-vested in local area, while a chain store only reinvests about 15 cents back into the community.

pride, and increased civic participation combine to provide clear opportunities for folks to work together for mutual benefit. From an environmental perspec-tive, by simply reducing the distance traveled to transport goods and resources some of the carbon footprint of the design supply chain can be mitigated. In short, local businesses can help improve the triple bottom line.

From another case study, Ecocreative's collaboration with the District Council of Mount Barker created a successful project that sourced local materials and talent. In their project, not only were the materials local, they were also sustainable. This emphasizes the importance of designers sourcing materials locally and working with nearby vendors who use renewable energy. Choosing materials manufac-tured with, and incorporating production processes fueled by, renewable energy will minimize the need to drill or extract oil from tar sands, deep from under the ocean floor, or next to sensitive wildlife areas. Similar to how choosing local helps raise median income, if, in the United States, we increase our renewable energy production to 25%, that same amount of electricity (from fossil fuels) can create up to three times more jobs.[7] However, as we all know, this isn't the case yet. The dependency on fossil fuels for graphic design work is pervasive. Printing inks and finishes are petroleum-based. Paper and pulping mills, printing presses, and data hosting centers require a lot of energy to function. Computers and other technologies used throughout the design process along with shipping raw mate-rials and finished designed products necessitate burning oil, coal, and natural gas. All of the steps in the current process lead to deforestation, create pollution, and hasten the rate at which our climate is warming. This linear and destructive design process must change.

But how can a designer on the job help support this necessary step in our pro-fession's transformation? The market follows consumer demand and increases or decreases supply accordingly. Divesting from oil and coal and investing in renewables is just one way to speed up a societal shift away from a dirty carbon culture to one that is more clean and healthy. By choosing petroleum-based inks or materials from across the globe, one supports a carbon-based economy—the opposite of what is needed. As designers, we are all connected to this problem and indirectly responsible for the mess our decisions can make. Instead of working with vendors who rely on fossil fuel for energy, we can avoid another catastrophic oil spill like the BP Deepwater Horizon or *Exxon Valdez* and work with vendors that support and use renewable energy. As comedian Bill Maher sarcastically said, "You know what happens when windmills collapse into the sea? A splash."

## Learn about materials and manufacturing

This seemingly obvious bit of advice may be among the most important, and the most time consuming. This is why the designers at Cast Iron Design equate sustainability research to investigative journalism and comment that extra time is needed in a systems thinking process to ensure you have explored not only the bigger picture but also the details. This is not time wasted, however. The knowledge gained from learning about materials and manufacturing processes are valuable to help educate clients and stakeholders and for making sound design decisions. It is also useful to help inform and inspire other designers to embark on the path toward sustainability. As the gatekeepers who stand in between the client and the consumer, graphic designers can control what enters the world, good or bad. Question "what is good?" and find ways to make that happen.

La PAGE designers also recommend asking manufacturers about the origin of all possible materials and design for recyclability or reuse once the materials are not in use. This involves systems thinking and mapping the type of possible materials, their geographic locations, and impacts of each. This initially takes time, but once you acquire information about a material or other designers share that knowledge with each other, the mapping and decision-making processes will go faster.

In general, virgin materials should be replaced with predominantly post-consumer ones that renourish our society and planet. For example, designers Jesvin Yeo and Alving Ng at Designing Cultures Studio advise using materials that are made from raw ingredients that grow quickly—like bamboo. Agricultural residues like wheat straw have a quick growing cycle and can be turned into paper products that have a considerably smaller environmental footprint when compared with tree fibers. Wheat straw, which has less than half the environmental footprint of 100% virgin tree fiber paper,[8] is also becoming a popular substitute for tree fiber paper with mills in operation or being launched in India, Canada, and the Pacific Northwest of the United States. Going forward, designers can tackle the concept of "to renourish" by growing fiber for paper through the planting of native grasses in areas that need soil remediation (brownfields) with additional compost to clean and improve soil. Also, with smarter crop rotation, farmers can grow food like wheat during one season and then canola the next or plant winter cover crops (between growing seasons) like vetch, oats, or rye to add much needed nitrogen to the soil, improve the soil's ability to hold water, and control weeds (avoiding fertilizers, pesticides, and river runoff). The waste from all of these plants can be turned into commercial paper products—which can also help support farmers. This paper and packaging can be collected later and used as compost (to also improve soil) or recycled (with the right municipal multistream recovery system)—leaving trees standing. This is becoming ever more important. The designer as a citizen must increasingly support processes that sequester the carbon from our atmosphere to slow the negative repercussions of global warming.

## Minimize materials and design backward

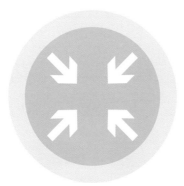

When design projects take the form of physical objects, it's important to remember the familiar 1970 mantra of "reduce, reuse, and recycle." At a glance, it's easy to notice that "reduce" comes first in the slogan and actually for a really good reason. While recycling is advertised and promoted the most out of the "Three R's" as an eco-friendly exercise, it is reduction where emphasis should be placed. Reducing material used, from a basic perspective, can save the client money and, in turn, reduce waste and negative environmental or social impacts. However, there are even more critical reasons to minimize the amount of material that is used in print, exhibition, or signage projects. The reduction of material usage is paramount due to growing global populations, consequent increased consumption and waste, and dwindling new resources. It is worth remembering as well that our planet is warming, which will create extreme shifts in weather, temperature, and rainfall (as we're already seeing in various parts of the Western United States, Australia, and Brazil) making access to food and other natural resources difficult and more expensive. Naomi Klein, in her 2014 book *This Changes Everything* urges a return for wealthy Western nations to the consumption levels of the 1970s (falling in line with our hippie mantra) to slow our carbon emissions and rising global temperatures. Questioning the initial project outcomes, choosing vendors that use renewable energy, and minimizing material use and waste are just three connected ways graphic designers can help to improve our planet.

From a different case study, Swerve Design shared how they minimized materials by considering which printed formats and sizes would use the least amount of resources. Cast Iron Design found that allowing the size of the press sheet to determine the dimensions of the print piece is helpful to minimize trim waste and help stay under budget. Today, they specifically use the Re-nourish online "Project Calculator" to size all their print projects efficiently for the press sheet. Lisa Hemingway at Backyard Creative uses the same method to consider the end of the project lifecycle first. She considers where the project will "die" and designs in reverse. This concept is called "designing backward." Designer Brian Dougherty uses this phrase to describe his studio Celery Design's creative process and explained it in detail in his 2008 book *Green Graphic Design*. Dougherty's book has clearly inspired many designers from our case studies and his method of designing backward is a practical strategy to follow while making detailed decisions about your project in your systems map.

Be passionate and excited about creating a more responsible outcome

Enthusiasm is contagious. Any designer that has ever successfully pitched a project understands that when you love what you do, and the more passionate and convincing you are, the more likely the client is to jump on board. This rings true when it comes to educating a client about designing sustainably. Enthusiasm helps make a presentation and a message much more powerful because that energy comes through in your body language and in what you say. Edward Morris from The Canary Project explains that people respond to emotional dedication, suggesting that designers can explain why the ethics of sustainable design align with the values of the client. When the designer and the client are working together toward a common objective, it is highly likely to be successful and sustainable.

This enthusiasm about sustainability can also "add considerable value to your design practice," according to Cast Iron Design. They believe that sustainability is "an exciting pursuit that provides an immediate sense of accomplishment and satisfaction." As designers, we have an obligation to improve lives through the things that we make. When a design project is completed sustainably, designers can take pride knowing that they are stewards of the earth and control the ways in which they impact people, the planet, and the economy.

Enthusiasm also intensifies focus. The competitive nature of many designers pushes us to continue to improve and step forward with each project until someday the profession of graphic design is working to renourish our world, its people, and all living things.

## Build trust and stay true to values

Building trust is a crucial requirement in sustaining any professional relationship, whether it is about creating confidence and loyalty on the end-user side or establishing rapport between the designer and the client (or supervisor). With the latter, it is crucial that when trying to convince a client to work together toward sustainable design solutions that they have faith in you and your ideas. As you may recall, our first step in the woven circular model of systems thinking is to "listen to the client and collectively determine project goals." This is a vital first step to build a lasting professional relationship and to understand the goals and values of both parties. Architect William McDonough believes in putting values first. Doing so helps businesses "set purposeful goals and seek continuous improvement in everything they do."[9] It is important to learn about the client's values and adhere to them throughout the process. Studio EMMI also finds this to be true and suggests to "(f)ind out what really matters to the client (not just what they have requested in the brief)." As designers, we can honor our clients' values, possibly even building on them, and work to follow those values through their visual communication.

In the case study from Cast Iron Design's Jonny Black, he explains that the key to a good client/designer relationship is trust fostered by honesty, kindness, thoroughness, and by genuinely caring about the client's goals and mission. Once that trust was established, he explains, "the rest was easy."

## Challenge existing processes and project constraints

This piece of advice was the most popular among the designers highlighted in this book. Designers from Modern Species, Swerve Design, Studio EMMI, Metalli Lindberg, and Ecocreative all suggest asking questions and learning about where and how your design solutions will live and die. Be curious and ask as many questions as possible of clients and their stakeholders to learn about *why* a project needs to be created. Zooming out on the systems map to think about the big picture and potential impacts helps inform more questions and inspire potential solutions. At the same time, our design process should always include a research phase that informs the brainstorming. These ideas should be discussed, revamped, and explored in detail to determine their potential positive and negative impacts. (From our "Powers of Ten" example in Chapter 2, this step is visualized as zooming in.) Furthermore, as you weave back and forth between idea generation, discussion, and analysis, "be curious" as both studios Modern Species and Metalli Lindberg suggest. By finding out what really matters to the client and what they are trying to achieve—beyond what has been requested in the brief—might lead to alternative, more effective, and sustainable solutions than what the client initially brought to the table.

## There will be tradeoffs

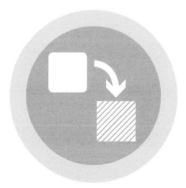

When a successful project does happen, it's wonderful; however, making it happen on the first try is not always possible, particularly when working toward sustainability. Often, there will be compromises or tradeoffs. But designers can use these opportunities to push the boundaries of their own creativity and problem-solving skills, as partner and creative director Gage Mitchell at Modern Species did in his Qet Botanicals project. The original goal for the packaging design was to eliminate the box altogether but there was no way to fit all the necessary information on the smaller bottles. Instead, the idea of a half-box emerged from ideation and discussion. The smaller box minimized material use and was made from 100% postconsumer waste–recycled paper that has all the trusted certifications like FSC, Green Seal, Green-e certified, and Processed Chlorine Free.

In another scenario, the positive social impact of a design solution may outweigh the possible negative environmental impacts resulting from the production or disposal of a design. For instance, one of the most effective ways to engage non-native speaking, low-income communities can be through printed materials. To promote a beneficial new government service to a low-income community, the most effective solution could be creating a brochure in several languages. The value of the design solution cannot be weighed independently from the purpose of the design. There is a tradeoff that occurs when considering the most effective method for communication with no simple solution. The choice to print thousands of brochures, as described in the example above, consumes natural resources, adds to pollution, and costs taxpayers' money. However, the end result educates the community about an important service that improves the standards of living and provides an important benefit for many. In this case, the designer can employ innovative ways to create and produce the brochure sustainably. The process can involve a give and take, and is often very challenging.

Tradeoffs are commonplace when designing for sustainability and take some creative problem-solving—a skill that just so happens to be the strength of graphic designers, although, sometimes it means piling on more work. Backyard Creative worked with two different printers in order to produce both pieces locally, and when Cast Iron Design could not find a suitable web hosting company powered by renewable energy, they recommended that their client purchase Renewable Energy Credits to offset the energy used in hosting their website. While the effectiveness of energy credits is highly debated, this was the next best alternative to using renewable energy in Cast Iron Design's situation. To ensure their energy uses would be covered with room to spare, they purchased more than four times the amount of credits necessary. Working to find suitable alternatives when the initial idea doesn't work takes dedication and passion (and if you've made it this far into the book, you've proven to have both traits).

Designers can create a better world, but it will require a shift in the process to systems thinking and a change in behavior. Designer Mike Montero, from Mule Design Studio in San Francisco, suggests that as designers, "we need to fear the consequences of our work more than we fear the consequences of speaking up" as "(we) are responsible for what (we) put into the world." Design, although not singularly, is largely responsible for increases in the speed of global warming, deforestation, pollution, and other ills; however, graphic designers can be an integral part of the solution.

## ENDNOTES

1. Orr, David W. 2004. *The Nature of Design: Ecology, Culture, and Human Intention.* Oxford University Press, Oxford, United Kingdom.
2. "The Multiplier Effect of Local Independent Businesses." n.d. *American Independent Business Alliance.* http://www.amiba.net/resources/multiplier-effect/. Accessed September 11, 2015.
3. This statistic is specific to the US, but similar results happen in other countries as well.
4. Neumark, David, Junfu Zhang, and Stephen Ciccarella. 2008. "The Effects of Wal-Mart on Local Labor Markets." *Journal of Urban Economics* 63 (2): 405–30.
5. Fleming, David A, and Stephan J. Goetz. 2011. "Does Local Firm Ownership Matter?" *Economic Development Quarterly* 25 (April): 277–81. doi:10.1177/0891242411407312.
6. Blanchard, Troy C., Charles Tolbert, and Carson Mencken. 2011. "The Health and Wealth of US Counties: How the Small Business Environment Impacts Alternative Measures of Development." *Cambridge Journal of Regions, Economy, and Society* 8. doi:10.1093/cjres/rsr034v1.
7. "Benefits of Renewable Energy Use." n.d. *Union of Concerned Scientists.* http://www.ucsusa.org/clean_energy/our-energy-choices/renewable-energy/public-benefits-of-renewable.html#.V6Ol-WXwzrk. Accessed September 11, 2015.
8. Offsetters. 2014. "Expanded Comparative Life Cycle Study of Wheat Straw Paper." *Step Forward Paper.* http://stepforwardpaper.com/wp-content/uploads/2014/10/SFP-life-cycle-study-final-141009.pdf. Accessed September 11, 2015.
9. McDonough, William. "Driving Sustainable Transformation via the Power of Design." *The Guardian.* August 19, 2013. https://www.theguardian.com/sustainable-business/sustainable-transformation-power-design. Accessed September 11, 2015.

# Chapter 6
## TOMORROW

"Don't stop thinking about tomorrow, Don't stop, it'll soon be here," sang Fleetwood Mac in 1977; however, as we save drafts of this book to the cloud, while receiving real-time news on a smartwatch millions of times more powerful than the Apollo Guidance Computer (AGC) in 1969, it seems like we're living in the future *now*. It makes us wonder what lies ahead for us as graphic designers. Our case studies highlight some great practical and inspirational strategies for designing more sustainably today, but how will they change in the approaching decades? If anyone were required to accurately predict the future of the profession, they would have a difficult time doing so. The incredibly quick technological advances in computing that has taken place over the past 30 years have helped the world become a lot more connected and consequently socially aware. This current "information age" has allowed designers to explore new areas to use their expertise, make more money (for some), and expand their skillsets beyond simply print, signage, and branding. Graphic design has changed drastically since the days of only controlling where ink falls on paper. Many design visionaries in 1996 would be hard pressed to imagine the world as it is now—mobile apps and devices, cloud computing, social media, and most importantly how we, as designers, have helped to damage our planet.

Hopefully, your design studies would have introduced you to Victor Papanek (who we quoted in Chapter 1) whose work dates further back than the past 30 years to the 1960s. He may not have been able to predict how fast technology has changed and influenced our profession, but 50 years ago he was able to get a few other things right. He wrote in *Design for the Real World* that "... by creating whole species of permanent garbage to clutter up the landscape, and by choosing materials and processes that pollute the air we breathe, designers have become a dangerous breed." He also suggested that "(d)esign, if it is to be ecologically responsible and socially responsive, must be revolutionary and radical."[1] Both thoughts are indeed *radical* and sadly a wake-up call that in the 1960s went largely ignored. But effects of global warming are difficult to ignore now—the extreme weather happening all over the globe is nature's air horn blasting in our ears to pay attention, to evolve.

It's fair to say then that the future of graphic design is intrinsically tied to how society chooses to tackle not only global warming but also the growing divide between the extremely wealthy and the poor. Designer and educator Bernard Canniffe passionately lectures on the designers' connection not only to the economy but also to the members of the community. His work shows quite well that "graphic design needs the middle class." The middle class makes up the bulk of the population in the United States (where Re-nourish is located) and has been the backbone of labor and economic growth for decades. However, as writer Aimee Pichi explains in lieu of quite sobering 2013 statistics that, "(i)f the middle-class is the economic backbone of America, then the country is developing osteoporosis."[3] Sustainability can only occur when there is balance in the triple bottom line of people, profit, and planet. This means that society must remedy the income gap. Equity is a must.

We believe that the destiny of graphic design is, yes, tied to what happens with technology, culture, economy, and environment. And considering the facts before us, we feel strongly that systems thinking is the best process to design in harmony with nature. The last part of this book describes our own detailed and sometimes lofty predictions for the graphic designer as a creative person and also as a citizen.

## A RADICAL TRANSITION

Systems thinking is the path forward. It is the only current conceivable way to continue designing effectively. The design process must align to biomimicry. The outcomes must strive to make lives better keeping in mind that readability, beauty, and usability aren't the only elements that make design work prolific. Outcomes that help the client keep the air and water clean, the planet free of burning fossil fuels, are affordable and fairly sourced, are manufactured locally under safe working conditions, and contribute to gender equity and in general higher pay are "good design." Along the way, this would require minimizing and choosing materials from waste streams, creating work that lasts longer and can be later reused, recycled, or upcycled. Clearly, creating a digital experience would avoid the use of materials from the perspective of the graphic designer, but it would not absolve designers of responsibility. Energy (from hosting), impact of experience, user privacy, accessibility, and usability are all pivotal to an outcome that attempts to balance the triple bottom line. Achieving this lofty goal requires a better understanding of our complex profession, its audiences, and the potential positive and negative impacts of the work. Systems thinking provides an opportunity by co-designing with clients to map out the audience(s), materials, vendors, and potential design outcomes while zooming in and out of each to find a balanced triple bottom line result to instruct the final design decision.

This future of graphic design will evolve from a radical transition for sure. However, it is one that is needed. As Papanek described design work as permanent garbage that pollutes the air and land, designers can instead create work that does the opposite—causes no harm and improves lives. Humanity is *not* stronger than Mother Earth. Naomi Klein argues that "our economic system and our planetary system are now at war."[4] In other words, the way all economies (and consequently design) function in which overconsumption and infinite growth are worshipped is not only unsustainable but also literally in opposition to one another. The way design is created and consumed will have to change now, not sometime down the line. This will take everyone, and it means (as you saw in the case studies) that you individually can make a difference one design decision at a time.

Design must course correct to choose renewable energy vendors in addition to a new and more effective design processes via systems thinking. Already the design school at Carnegie Mellon has completely overhauled its entire design curriculum to focus on what they call "Transitional Design." They hope this new design education will help to prepare and empower future designers for the changes ahead. Carnegie Mellon has readily made their entire educational materials online and open-sourced[5] for other design educators across the world to share experiences and learn different ways to teach systems thinking to their students.

## OPEN-SOURCE KNOWLEDGE SHARING

Education is precisely where this great transition should start. Systems thinking should be taught in colleges and universities; however, if you have already completed your degree (and will miss out on this training), there is obviously another way to learn—on the job. Friends working next to you and remotely have much to offer and it's often through colleagues that information is shared. Lessons learned, like those from the case studies in this book, are prime examples of how knowledge is shared with one another as new projects begin. As pointed out earlier, those who are transitioning their design process to think in systems will most likely find they need to add additional time for client projects at the outset (something, of course, many clients don't like to hear). What is needed is open-source, online (and books like this one) depositories of best practices, vendors, materials, and discussion forum that can be used to avoid pitfalls and save precious time spent researching and problem-solving issues other designers/agencies have experienced. From our case studies, we learned that Cast Iron Design "... spent dozens of extra hours researching cotton production, woven label production, eco binding options for journals, 100% recycled corrugated box sourcing, recyclability of various adhesive packaging tapes, and so on." This was a definite investment for their client, but in the end, the information gathered could also be shared with the design community. The great news is that Re-nourish, the Living Principles, and other resource-driven initiatives are platforms for open-source knowledge that have helped lead the way for websites like the recently launched National Materials Marketplace. This pilot project is a joint venture led by the Corporate Eco Forum (CEF), United States Business Council for Sustainable Development (US BCSD), and the World Business Council for Sustainable Development (WBCSD) to connect international companies with an online database that helps customers reuse or exchange materials and to help establish a revolving supply chain.[6] This type of online resource can help eliminate waste, reuse and recycle materials, cut costs, reduce carbon footprint, and hopefully speed up the educational process on how to design using systems thinking. However, our online resources can be larger than simply a virtual marketplace to buy/sell reused or recycled materials, they can also feature a means for sharing and discussing best practices for implementing systems thinking.

## MORE EXPERIENCE-BASED OUTCOMES

The future discussed so far in this section exclusively involves only the physical outputs as a profession. The planet's damaged biological systems combined with the dire consequences resulting from global warming demand that we all produce and consume less stuff. This includes the amount of physical work that's done. This is clearly controversial and not something anyone, including us, wants to hear; however, a forecasted 4°C global temperature increase by the end of the 21st century will be devastating to our global community. Designers can decide to design a better tomorrow today or precariously wait and let this current path literally pave the way for us. The latter will be catastrophic. This points to imminent changes for the graphic design profession. Looking ahead, we believe experiences will matter more than objects. Recent psychological studies have shown that spending money on experiences "provide(s) more enduring happiness" than purchasing a product.[7] Creating fleeting moments whether good or bad, finds psychology Professor Thomas Gilbert, generate more happiness and better stories that help to improve the construction of individual identities and personal connections with others. The graphic designer already does create experiences digitally within the service and branding industries. The sense of interaction and joy (hopefully) one feels from using a web or mobile app or the sense of excitement an audience feels while watching the captivating opening credits of a film are two examples of many that define experiential design. Also, branding which traditionally was logotypes and taglines on printed brochureware is now defined by the customer experience whether it be in a store or online. No longer only focused on what the customers see, branding is now about what people feel when interacting or thinking about a brand. These experiences can be more lasting, fulfilling, and memorable if the designer involves not just the client but also the user in a more collaborative design process. Many design studios like IDEO and Frog are well-versed in user-centered design and provide great online toolkits to help enhance and develop an effective design experience. Using these resources and improving upon them through trial and error will only help navigate the profession forward.

Already there is an example of what could be part of the future in the recent growth in the sharing economy—or the reuse of excess goods, skills, space, services, or even money. Companies like Airbnb, Etsy, Kickstarter, and Freecycle use design successfully to help create revenue streams sharing or reusing goods and services. Usually nothing physical is actually created in this experience, which does help the triple bottom line in many ways. Design in the sharing economy reduces consumption of new items while still adding revenue into the economy, allows access to services to many who can't afford them otherwise, and also helps reduce dangerous greenhouse gas emissions from manufacture and transport of new goods. And if you recall the importance of the local multiplier effect, you'll recognize that sharing resources locally will also help improve the community much more effectively.

It's also important to note that creating great experiences will require energy to power. It may also mean needing connected objects and printed or digital campaigns for folks to know that this experience exists. If physical ephemera are needed as part of an experience, they will hopefully be designed and manufactured with strategies like the ones learned from our case studies to help achieve sustainability. At any rate, the first step to thinking in systems that we proposed earlier is still valid in creating an enduring experience—knowing the most effective outcome for the goals of the project. Asking more strategic, poignant, and informed questions of the client is a vital part to move beyond pre-determined outcomes allowing the discussion to open up to the possibility of designing for an experience or service. Then, including those potential outcomes and audiences in your systems map while also researching their impacts are crucial to thinking in systems as a designer.

## OUR COLLECTIVE AND INDIVIDUAL VALUES

*The notion that science will save us is the chimera that allows the present generation to consume all the resources it wants, as if no generations will follow it. It is the sedative that allows civilization to march so steadfastly toward environmental catastrophe. It forestalls the real solution, which will be in the hard, nontechnical work of changing human behavior.*

—**Kenneth Brower**[8]

However, before any real transition can happen, the graphic design community together and individually must reflect upon on our values. Designers as citizens have an obligation to be respectful to all fellow human beings and to the planet we share. As a collective, designers must ask what issues are important? What do we want to make and why? What are the ethics of the design profession and consequently how do they affect the planet, economy, and society? If sustainability is a high priority, it will mean a transition that necessitates rethinking of what is being made and the way in which design is practiced and approached.

This will be difficult. Should designers decide between making a decent paycheck or designing only for clients with ethical compatibility to themselves? Should designers refuse to take on a project unless the client does business in a way that supports social and environmental initiatives? The short answer is no. While some of the most enjoyable and rewarding work can be for good causes, making a living and having a responsible design practice do not need to be mutually exclusive. The designers in Chapter 4 have outlined practical lessons on how to design to improve the triple bottom line while working with clients. Our systems thinking process can help plot out that course and also be a visual reference point throughout the process. There is no need to turn away freelance work or quit your job when a request comes in to develop chewing gum packaging, for example. Instead, you can think and design in systems to direct the focus of your work toward a positive impact. Yes, even with designing chewing gum wrappers.

Professional graphic design organizations like Society of Graphic Designers of Canada (GDC) and the AIGA (The Professional Association for Design) both propose standards of professional practice that define the expectations of their member's actions toward ethical behavior and socially and environmentally responsible design. The standards are a suggestion, however, and paying membership dues does not bind a designer to adhere to these organizations' values.

So how do designers join forces and design for the greater good when there are no current guidelines, rules, or checks and balances? Does the future of design require something like a physician's Hippocratic Oath where designers pledge to do no harm? Canadian graphic designers can apply to become GDC certified indicating a high level of professional standard has been met as well as pledging a commitment to an ethical and sustainable practice as outlined by the GDC. Perhaps, there is a possibility where designers worldwide, much like electricians or architects, must be registered and certified in order to practice professionally. Before becoming certified, a graphic designer would be required to complete rigorous sustainability training and subsequent follow-up training as new technologies emerge and discoveries are made. There could be a metrics in which to quantify the impacts of design work, similar to the way LEED certification measures the impacts of buildings, interiors, and neighborhoods for both sustainability and community benefits. With this system for graphic design, there is hope that all design work would be measured against a set of standards regarding environmental, social, and financial impacts plainly accessible to the public for ultimate transparency. It would be important with any sort of certification that the emphasis is placed on impact and not aesthetics limiting a designer's creative freedom. Deregulate imagination!

## DESIGN TO RENOURISH

The sustainable design discussion seems to usually focus on the notion of reducing the negative impacts of designed outcomes. Designers hear that by using recycled paper and vegetable-based inks, they're "saving the environment" or by leaving a female model's blemish un-Photoshopped they're boosting women's collective self-esteem. Actions like these do indeed help graphic design move closer to becoming more sustainable (so keep on doing them!), but they still have a negative environmental, social, or financial impact—just *less* so.

The title of this book, we believe, is also a part of the future for graphic designers. Design to renourish means that design outcomes and process could work not only to minimize negative consequences but instead, and even better, create positive effects. This is a future where graphic design work improves and replenishes resources—in other words, that chewing gum package adds value to the triple bottom line in having been made.

Designing to renourish is not a new idea generally—being only slightly more common in other design fields like industrial, product, and furniture design— but it still hasn't been applied to the design profession in a significant way. Herman Miller has numerous Cradle to Cradle Certified$^{CM}$ products in its furniture lines that epitomize the idea of design to renourish. Each part of these products can be easily replaced, recycled, or put back into the system to create new parts. Their furniture is not only safe from harmful chemicals and processes but Herman Miller is also on a path to becoming carbon neutral by 2020 and currently uses 100% renewable energy in all their facilities. The goal in truly sustainable design is to "close the loop" where nothing becomes waste. This is done by using materials that can either be recycled into new products or returned to nature through composting.

Similar to Herman Miller, Gavin Munro, from Derbyshire, England, makes chairs. Instead of cutting down trees for the lumber, he grows, trains, and grafts small trees to grow into chairs. Munro avoids much of the greenhouse gas emissions from typical furniture making, instead allows his growing chairs to absorb carbon dioxide, prevent soil erosion, provide shelter for wildlife, and add beauty to his outdoor factory—a farm. Branches from each tree are trained to grow into a plastic form of a chair he designed; once ready, the branches are pruned to "harvest" the chair. The tree can be used again as it is not cut down. Instead, it is only pruned, so any new shoots can be trained to make a new chair. Now imagine for a moment if these very same principles could be applied to graphic design work!

Gaining in popularity, the concept of repurposing waste is another approach to sustainable design. Today, with landfill space busting at the seams and the price of new materials increasing, companies are figuring out ways to reuse this abundant resource—waste. United Airlines is developing a better jet fuel using oils extracted from animal and vegetable fats from household trash. While the environmental footprint of air travel is hefty, using garbage as fuel can help mitigate the economic and environmental impact of flying. The airline company is now preparing to construct a facility that will produce about 10 million gallons of ethanol annually using household garbage.[9]

Clothing companies like Patagonia and Outerknown are already ahead of the game when it comes to making new products from trash. Sustainable practices have been a mainstay in Patagonia's mission. Their pledge to corporate responsibility and environmental advocacy led them, as early as 1993, to create a fleece jacket from recycled plastic soda bottles. Now recycled content can be found in many of their clothing products.[10] Outerknown, founded by pro-surfer Kelly Slater, includes 100% recyclable clothing made from reclaimed fishing nets, carpet, and other nylon waste from the Pacific Garbage Patch.[11] An intriguing quality of nylon is that it can be broken down and re-born an infinite amount of times into new clothing, while still keeping the same quality as a fabric. Kelly Slater is designing one way to help clean up the ocean from its plastic nightmare and turn that into a sustainable clothing company—closing the loop.

When applying these very same principles to graphic design, we can find ways to turn "trash into treasure" and create materials that can be infinitely recycled, upcycled, or composted (think agricultural fibers) so that the things we create continue to provide nourishment for healthy growth. Because the work we do as designers affects living systems, graphic designers can create in innovative ways to make those systemic impacts positive. If humans continue to believe that they hold dominion over nature as we have done for three centuries, we will leave an inhospitable mess for future generations. Our legacy as a people and designers will be an unlivable planet (with a struggling economy) that no longer provides clean air, water, and abundant resources. Because we, as a society, are idle or too stubborn, future generations will inherit a planet that will make them sicker. Design must work to improve the triple bottom line. To do this, nature must be the example, where waste equals food (as Bill McDonough and Michael Braungart famously proposed). In nature, waste like fallen flower petals and seed casings are nourishment for more things to grow. (Remember the hawk, the squirrel, and the oak tree?) It makes sense then that designers can use this as a guide, so that when a designed piece is no longer needed, it provides the materials for new products or it delivers nourishment to the soil for new growth. Only by following nature's systems can the profession design to renourish.

We firmly believe the idea of designing to renourish is not far-fetched. The inspiration to make it happen is all around us in nature. Blogs, magazines, conferences, exhibitions, and books provide designers with a lot of inspiration for beautiful new work but nature is the model for a process to build. Nature works through a complex network of interconnected systems that are self-perpetuating and healthy (when humans don't get involved). It is logical, then, that creating and thinking in systems is the right way to design. As we combat global warming, wealthier economies need to produce and consume less (as other nations grow—as sustainability also includes equity) altering not only how but what we create. Designed experiences in a sharing economy, we believe, will be a big part of our future. But whatever our future holds, we can and will build a stronger design community together through this journey—and you won't be alone. Resources like re-nourish.org are places to share and learn from others about systems thinking. In-person meetups and social media like Twitter and Facebook are also perfect for swapping tips and inspiration. The momentum will be contagious. This paradigm shift will also require allies, clients, and partners to work together. Designers must change, and it will, of course, be a challenge. We must act together now to make our design work sustainable as global warming will not wait. This is the mission and it starts today. Onward!

# ENDNOTES

1. Papanek, Victor. 2005. *Design for the Real World: Human Ecology and Social Change*. 2nd ed. Chicago Review Press, Chicago, IL.

2. These statistics are from the Pew Charitable Trust and show a considerable drop in families still in the middle class since 2000. In some of the worst cases, there are losses of up to 5%. http://www.pewtrusts.org/en/research-and-analysis/blogs/stateline/2015/3/19/the-shrinking-middle-class-mapped-state-by-state. Accessed September 25, 2015.

3. Picchi, Aimee. 2015. "America's Incredible Shrinking Middle Class." *CBS News*. March 23. http://www.cbsnews.com/news/americas-incredible-shrinking-middle-class/. Accessed September 25, 2015.

4. Klein, Naomi. 2015. *This Changes Everything: Capitalism vs. The Climate*. Reprint edition. Simon & Schuster, New York, NY, p. 21.

5. You can locate these Transitional Design course materials online at https://www.academia.edu/13122242/Transition_Design_Overview. This site will require setting up a free account to view any resources. Accessed September 25, 2015.

6. "New Online Marketplace Will Allow US Companies to Exchange Underutilized Materials." 2015. *Sustainable Brands*, July 8. http://www.sustainablebrands.com/news_and_views/next_economy/sustainable_brands/new_online_marketplace_will_allow_us_companies_exchan. Accessed September 25, 2015.

7. Kumar, Amit, Matthew A. Killingsworth, and Thomas Gilovich. 2014. "Waiting for Merlot: Anticipatory Consumption of Experiential and Material Purchases." *Psychological Science* 25 (10): 1924–31.

8. Brower, Kenneth. "The Danger of Cosmic Genius." *The Atlantic*. October 27, 2010. http://www.theatlantic.com/magazine/archive/2010/12/the-danger-of-cosmic-genius/308306/. Accessed September 25, 2015.

9. Phillips, Ari. 2015. "This Airline Just Invested Millions Into Turning Garbage Into Jet Fuel." *Think Progress*. July 3. http://thinkprogress.org/climate/2015/07/03/3676300/united-airplanes-powered-by-household-garbage. Accessed September 25, 2015.

10. n.d. *Patagonia*. http://www.patagonia.com/us/patagonia.go?assetid=2791. Accessed September 25, 2015

11. Chow, Lorraine. 2015. "Pro Surfer Kelly Slater Launches Clothing Line Made From Ocean Trash." *EcoWatch*, July 20. http://www.ecowatch.com/pro-surfer-kelly-slater-launches-clothing-line-made-from-ocean-trash-1882072696.html. Accessed September 25, 2015.

# APPENDIX

## RESOURCES

These resources are the ones we have curated and spent time personally investigating and vetting through external sources, and also match Re-nourish's own principles of transparency and actively move the design sustainability movement forward.

## PACKAGING

**GreenBlue**
www.greenblue.org

GreenBlue is an environmental nonprofit organization dedicated to the sustainable use of materials for designers. GreenBlue has made great strides in the use of healthier products and services for home, work, and recreation while promoting responsible use and material recovery.

**The Sustainable Packaging Coalition**
www.sustainablepackaging.org

The Sustainable Packaging Coalition (SPC) is a project of GreenBlue that is committed to the creation of environmentally and economically responsible packaging. They are the go to online resource for the most up-to-date information and strategies for sustainable packaging.

## PAPER AND PRINTING

**Canopy**
www.canopyplanet.org

Canopy is a nonprofit organization dedicated to protecting the environment. Together with their partners, Canopy helps create sustainable purchasing guidelines and develops comprehensive solutions that protect our forests. One of their biggest areas of focus currently is the promotion of agricultural fiber paper as the best alternative to tree fiber.

**Conservatree**

conservatree.org

Conservatree is a not-for-profit organization dedicated to providing fair and reasonable information about paper. They provide information for purchasing paper and paper reduction techniques, educational resources surrounding conservation and environmental issues, consulting, and recommendations for policymakers and legislators.

**Green Press Initiative**

www.greenpressinitiative.org

The Green Press Initiative works to advance awareness and provide education regarding the environmental and social impacts of the US book and newspaper industries. They deliver toolkits for publishers and printers to help start responsible environmental policies to aid in this advancement of greener presses.

**Environmental Paper Network**

environmentalpaper.org

The Environmental Paper Network (EPN) is a reliable and credible voice on pulp and paper sustainability. The EPN is a network of over 100 organizations working for social justice and conservation presented by the expanding forest, pulp, and paper industry.

## DIGITAL

**Green Certified Site**

www.co2stats.com

Green Certified Site™ is a web badge that calculates a website's environmental footprint, provides suggestions for making a website more energy efficient, and automatically offsets the site's carbon footprint through contributions to wind and solar farms. While the benefits of carbon offsets are heavily debated (see "Carbon Offsetting" in the Terms and Definitions section), there are multiple other beneficial tools offered through this resource.

**The World Wide Web Consortium**

www.w3.org

The World Wide Web Consortium (W3C) is an international community that develops open standards to ensure the long-term growth of the web that is accessible to all. One of W3C's primary goals is to make the benefits of the web available to all people, whatever their hardware, software, network infrastructure, native language, culture, geographical location, or physical or mental ability.

## CERTIFICATIONS

**Ancient Forest Friendly**

canopyplanet.org/ancientforest

This certification is among the most reliable paper designations available. Ancient forest-friendly paper is chlorine-free, includes no ancient or endangered forest fiber, and is made with a high percentage of recycled or straw paper content. Any virgin tree fiber used must be certified by the Forest Stewardship Council (FSC). One can be assured that ancient forest-friendly paper is among the most sustainable papers on the market.

**B Corporation**

www.bcorporation.net

B Corp certification is a third-party certification requiring companies to meet social sustainability and environmental performance standards, and accountability standards. Certified B Corps (which currently total over 1,000) offer a positive vision of a better way to do business by creating benefits for all stakeholders, not just shareholders. They believe the global economy can be a force for good if businesses do no harm and benefit all.

**Blue Angel**

www.blauer-engel.de

The Blue Angel is a German environmental label that guarantees that a product or service meets high standards when it comes to its environmental, health, and performance characteristics. In the process, these products and services are always evaluated across their entire life cycle. In order to reflect technological advances, the Federal Environmental Agency reviews these criteria every three to four years. This process requires companies to constantly improve the environmental friendliness of their products over time.

**Business for Social Responsibility**

www.bsr.org

The mission of Business for Social Responsibility (BSR) is to work with business to create a just and sustainable world. BSR's role is to catalyze change within business by integrating sustainability into strategy and operations, and to promote collaboration among companies and their stakeholders for systemic progress. Like B Corporation, they believe that the "role of business is to create and deliver products and services in a way that treats people fairly, meets individuals' needs and aspirations within the boundaries of our planet, and encourages market and policy frameworks that enable a sustainable future."

## Chlorine Free Product Association

www.chlorinefreeproducts.org

The Chlorine Free Products Association (CFPA) is a trustworthy, independent not-for-profit accreditation and standard setting organization. They focus on promoting sustainable manufacturing practices, implementing advanced technologies free of chlorine chemistry, educating consumers on alternatives, and developing world markets for sustainably produced third-party-certified products and services.

## Cradle to Cradle Products Innovation

www.c2ccertified.org

Cradle to Cradle Products Innovation is an open-sourced product and materials certification system developed by McDonough Braungart Design Chemistry (MBDC). Cradle to Cradle or C2C-certified materials meet the following basic criteria:

- Made using environmentally safe and healthy materials
- Designed for recycling or composting
- Produced with renewable energy, and energy and water efficiency
- Incorporates strategies for social responsibility

Cradle to Cradle[SM] also refers to a design system in which products are created within closed loops, resulting in a waste-free manufacturing process. Material inputs and outputs are seen either as technical or biological nutrients; technical nutrients can be recycled or reused with no loss of quality, while biological nutrients can be composted or consumed.

## Consumer Product Safety Commission

http://www.cpsc.gov

The Consumer Product Safety Commission is an American governmental safety agency that reports to the United States Congress. They aim to protect the public from unreasonable risks of injury or death associated with the use of thousands of consumer products under the agency's jurisdiction.

## EcoLabel

www.ec.europa.eu/environment/ecolabel/index_en.htm

The EU EcoLabel helps designers identify products and services that have a reduced environmental impact throughout their life cycle, from the extraction of raw material through to production, use, and disposal. Recognized throughout Europe, EU EcoLabel is a voluntary label promoting environmental excellence which can be trusted as it is set through a regulation of the European Parliament and of the Council, and the criteria are developed and revised in a transparent way by a group of experts and stakeholders.

### Eco Logo

www.industries.ul.com/environment/certificationvalidation-marks/ecologo-product-certification

Eco Logo is a popular North American environmental labeling program that incorporates life-cycle analysis originally developed by the Canadian government and now managed by UL, a global independent science safety company. Although a paid certification system (with fees in the $1,500–$5,000 range), the EcoLabel is widely accepted as a valid labeling system that meets ISO 14024 standards.

### Forest Stewardship Council

www.ic.fsc.org

The Forest Stewardship Council (FSC) is a certification system that provides standards and assurance that a wood product came from a sustainably managed forest. For a paper brand to be FSC Certified, it must follow what is called a "chain of custody" process where the wood pulp was harvested responsibly from a FSC-certified forest, produced by a FSC-certified mill, and finally given to a printer who is also FSC certified. Currently, FSC is the only widely accepted international certification program among independent environmental advocacy groups but not all FSC-certified papers are equal. The three main certifications are the 100% label, mixed sources label, and recycled label. The FSC is a positive step forward to prevent illegal logging and consequent deforestation by putting public pressure (through certification) on manufacturers to adhere to more stringent standards with their wood-based products.

### Green Seal

www.greenseal.org

Green Seal is a not-for-profit organization that uses life cycle–based sustainability standards to offer third-party certification for products, services, and companies. They hope to empower consumers, purchasers, and companies to create a more sustainable world.

### Green America

www.greenamerica.org/greenbusiness/certification.cfm

Green America is a membership-based not-for-profit organization that hopes "to harness economic power—the strength of consumers, investors, businesses, and the marketplace—to create a socially just and environmentally sustainable society." Green America focuses on economic action to solve social and environmental problems, empowers and mobilizes people to take action, works on social justice and environmental responsibility, and helps to stop abusive practices while creating healthy, just, and sustainable practices.

**Green-e**
www.green-e.org

Green-e is an independent consumer protection program monitoring the sale of renewable energy and greenhouse gas reductions in the retail market. Green-e offers certification and verification of renewable energy and greenhouse gas mitigation products and projects.

**ISO**
www.iso.org

International Organization for Standardization (ISO) is the world's largest developer and publisher of international standardization systems. ISO implements proprietary, industrial, and commercial standards worldwide.

ISO 14000 addresses "environmental management." This refers to what the organization does to minimize harmful effects to the environment caused by its activities, and to continually improve its environmental performance.

ISO 9000 addresses "quality management." This refers to what the organization does to fulfill quality requirements and applicable regulatory requirements while aiming to enhance customer satisfaction. The organization must also continue to improve its performance in pursuit of these objectives. Both of these are important factors that help to gauge the triple bottom line performance of a company.

**Rainforest Alliance**
www.rainforest-alliance.org

The Rainforest Alliance works to conserve biodiversity and ensure sustainable livelihoods by transforming land-use practices, business practices, and consumer behavior. They work with forward-thinking farmers, foresters, and tourism entrepreneurs to conserve natural resources and ensure the long-term economic health of forest communities. In order for a farm or forestry enterprise to achieve Rainforest Alliance certification, or for a tourism business to be verified, it must meet rigorous standards designed to protect ecosystems, safeguard the well-being of local communities, and improve productivity. The Rainforest Alliance then links these farmers, foresters, and tourism businesses to the growing global community of conscientious consumers through the green frog seal. Designers can look for this frog symbol and be rest assured that their paper choice is coming from a sustainable source.

**Occupational Safety and Health Administration**
www.osha.gov

Occupational Safety and Health Administration (OSHA) is an American governmental agency that was started with the passing of the Occupational Safety and Health Act in 1970. OSHA's directive from Congress is to assure safe and healthful working conditions for working men and women by setting and enforcing standards and by providing training, outreach, education, and assistance. If you are a designer outside of the United States, you should look for vendors that are certified by comparable organizations or governmental agencies.

### Sustainable Green Printing Partnership

sgppartnership.org

The Sustainable Green Printing Partnership (SGP) is a not-for-profit organization that provides a sustainable foundation by promoting best practices, networking, and innovation among raw material manufacturers, converters, printers, finishing facilities, trade associations, and print buyers. They are the leading certifier of North American printing facilities with an in-depth and affordable certification process.

## DESIGN RESOURCES

### Re-nourish

www.re-nourish.com

Re-nourish is a registered 501(c)(3) not-for-profit organization that provides online tools advocating awareness and action for systems thinking in the communication design community. Re-nourish believes that "good design" values people, the environment, and improves lives. Re-nourish aims to help the practicing communication designer, educator, and student make positive, greener, and pragmatic design decisions. Our tools and resources are created to be straightforward and implementable now. Our case studies, articles, and blogs provide inspiration and knowledge to help designers implement more sustainable strategies.

### Lovely as a Tree

lovelyasatree.com

Lovely as a Tree is a London-based organization that aims to enable and inspire British graphic designers to make more environmentally friendly choices in their work. Lovely as a Tree provides steps for reducing your design footprint, finding more sustainably sourced paper and printers, sourcing sustainable design case studies, and educating as to how to choose a greener printer.

### GreenBiz

www.greenbiz.com

GreenBiz is a content-rich online resource packed with articles, white papers, and webcasts for businesses and entrepreneurs. They hope to advance the opportunities at the intersection of business, technology, and sustainability, and promote the potential to drive transformation and accelerate progress—within companies, industries, and in the very nature of business.

**Inhabitat**

inhabitat.com

Inhabitat is a creative weblog devoted to the future of design, tracking the innovations in technology, practices, and materials that are pushing architecture and home design toward a smarter and more sustainable future. They provide daily inspirational content to connect the design community with the latest sustainable design innovations and projects.

**The Association of Registered Graphic Designers of Canada**

www.rgd.ca/resources/sustainability.php

The Association of Registered Graphic Designers of Canada (RGD) promotes the education and sharing of knowledge, research, advocacy, and mentorship. The RGD provides professional design standards and best practices in the profession and has adopted a sustainability policy on responsible design for people, planet, and profit.

**The Society for Experiential Graphic Design**

segd.org/explore/sustainability

The Society for Experiential Graphic Design (SEGD) is an association of designers "who create content-rich, emotionally compelling, experiential spaces for a wide range of environments, from hospitals and transit hubs to museums and educational campuses." This sustainability section of their site provides articles and tips for the experiential designer to incorporate into his or her daily practice.

**The Living Principles for Design**

livingprinciples.aiga.org

The Living Principles website and blog is a social platform where designers can co-create, share, and showcase best practices, tools, stories, and ideas for enabling sustainable action across all design disciplines. Beyond providing an online social space for designers to learn about and share their experiences with sustainability, The Living Principles also details a framework of environmental, social, economic, and cultural sustainability guidelines that can be woven into a graphic designers' daily practice.

# GLOSSARY

**Agricultural Residue**

The unused remains of food crops, such as wheat, flax, or corn, that are often disposed of by burning in the field, creating air pollution. In North America, million tons of agricultural residues are produced annually.[1] As a by-product of the primary food crop, agricultural residue does not add to the agricultural footprint or reduce the availability of food crops. Selling this fiber to paper mills can reduce air pollution, save trees by replacing wood fiber for making paper, and increase farm earnings. This is currently the most sustainable source for paper fiber and our favorite.

**Agri-Fiber Paper**

Paper made from nonwood agricultural fiber. These fibers fall into three main categories:

1. Dedicated fiber crops grown specifically for use in paper products such as hemp, bamboo, or kenaf.
2. Agricultural residues diverted from the farming waste stream (see definition of agricultural residues).
3. Industrial residues leftover as by-products of other fabrication processes.

Because each source of agri-fiber has different environmental requirements and impacts, there is no simple answer to the question, "which is better?" But choosing agri-fiber papers based on regional logistics can often reduce the environmental footprint of the project and is recommended as a potential area of savings.

**Biodegradable**

The ability of a substance to be broken down by biological agents, such as bacteria and other enzymes, into basic components. Although there is no universal definition or certification regarding biodegradability, the US Federal Trade Commission has issued the following guideline in its Guide for the Use of Environmental Marketing Claims: "A marketer making an unqualified degradable claim should have competent and reliable scientific evidence that the entire item will completely break down and return to nature (i.e., decompose into elements found in nature) within a reasonably short period of time after customary disposal."[2]

**Carbon Dioxide**

Carbon dioxide ($CO_2$) is a naturally occurring odorless and colorless gas in the earth's atmosphere. Together with other greenhouse gases (like methane and nitrous oxide), $CO_2$ contributes to climate change by absorbing the sun's natural radiation and reflecting it back to the earth's surface. Although $CO_2$

occurs naturally through processes like photosynthesis, human-caused $CO_2$ emissions have increased dramatically since the Industrial Revolution. The burning of fossil fuels, industrial manufacturing, and other everyday acts all contribute to increased carbon dioxide levels, in turn contributing to climate change.

**Carbon Footprint**
The total amount of greenhouse gases (carbon dioxide, methane, nitrous oxide, hydrofluorocarbons, perfluorocarbons, and sulfur hexafluoride) emitted over the full life cycle of a product, service, organization, or individual. Carbon footprints in the era of global warming are to be avoided; however, getting to know an exact footprint is challenging as calculations vary wildly, but the most commonly accepted standard is the Greenhouse Gas (GHG) Protocol developed by the World Resources Institute and the World Business Council for Sustainable Development. Simplified calculators to aid self-awareness are available from Climate Crisis and the Environmental Protection Agency, but more rigorous methodologies like the GHG Protocol should be used for organizational reporting and decision-making.

**Carbon Neutrality**
The state of balancing one's carbon emissions with an equivalent in carbon offsets. The term is misleading, however, as it implies that one's greenhouse gas emissions can be rendered harmless by investing in an equivalent amount of offset units (see "Carbon Offsetting") and is often used to directly imply that a product or organization emits no greenhouse gases at all. Re-nourish discourages the use of the term on marketing materials or in messaging claims.

**Carbon Offsetting (or Carbon Credits)**
The act of investing in projects that reduces greenhouse gas production through the purchase of carbon offset units. A single carbon offset unit is equivalent to one metric ton of carbon dioxide (or its equivalent in other greenhouse gases). Individuals and organizations can purchase carbon offsets as a way of mitigating the carbon dioxide emissions resulting from everyday practices like travel, energy use, and waste disposal.

Typically, the money from carbon offsetting goes toward funding renewable energy, energy efficiency projects, or GHG sequestration. The US government regulates certain corporate carbon offsets through cap and trade agreements, while the voluntary offset market is growing.

There is much debate about the efficacy of carbon offsetting; proponents argue that it can help drive awareness by placing a monetary value on carbon emissions, while opponents argue that voluntary offset programs may actually increase carbon emissions by providing an excuse to consume more. Essentially, it can allow one company to buy the rights to pollute more from another and thereby not actually decrease, in the end, any carbon in the atmosphere.

**Clearcutting**

A process in which all trees in a selected area are felled in a logging operation. The effect on the environment can be extremely devastating due to the destruction of fire-preventing buffer zones; loss of habitat for animals, insects, and bacteria; increased global warming through release of carbon dioxide and loss of carbon sequestration; and soil erosion. Clearcutting often paves the way for converting the former native forest into farm land for monoculture, cattle rearing, or agriculture, thereby increasing the negative environmental and human impacts over clearcutting and replanting alone.

**e-Waste**

e-Waste, or electronic waste, refers to electronic devices that are near the end of their useful life and are classified as universal waste. Certain components of some electronic products contain hazardous contaminants, such as lead, mercury, cadmium, and beryllium, which when thrown away end up in landfills or incinerators. If informally processed, e-waste can cause serious health and pollution problems. Currently, electronic waste is one of the fastest growing components of our planet's waste stream.

**Greenhouse Gas**

Emitted gases that trap solar radiation, contributing to the destruction of the ozone layer and climate change. The most common greenhouse gases are those recognized by the 1997 Kyoto Protocol: carbon dioxide, methane, nitrous oxide, hydrofluorocarbons, perfluorocarbons, and sulfur hexafluoride.

**Greenwashing**

The act of misrepresenting one's behavior or product to appear more environmentally sound than it may in fact be. The term, derived from the words "green" (environmentally sound) and "whitewashing" (to conceal or gloss over wrongdoing), is generally applied when significantly more money or time has been spent advertising being eco-friendly, rather than actually implementing environmentally sound practices. Greenwashing can include focusing on one environmental benefit while ignoring the other harmful impacts, making unsubstantiated claims of being sustainable, or outright lying about environmental benefits or certifications.

**Leachate**

This is a toxic liquid that is produced when rainwater filters through landfill waste and reacts with the chemicals and other materials in the waste. Leachate can enter groundwater sources, posing significant environmental and health problems as a result.

**Life-Cycle Analysis**

Life-cycle analysis (LCA) is a technique to evaluate the environmental impacts associated with the creation of a product, process, or service. LCA is assessed by inventory analysis, impact analysis, and improvement analysis where material inputs and environmental outputs are thoroughly examined. There are software and companies that specialize in this analysis.

**Monoculture Plantation**
The practice of growing one single crop over a wide area. In forestry, it refers to the planting of one species of tree crop without biodiversity. To ensure that only one species of trees grow, the trees are usually sprayed with harsh chemicals, contaminating local waterways and communities with devastating effects on wildlife and human health. Monoculture is rarely good for our natural environment.

**Post-Consumer Waste**
Paper or paper products that have reached the consumer before being discarded and collected again for recycling. For example, paper and cardboard collected from a curbside recycling program are considered to be post-consumer waste (PCW). PCW paper products have a longer life cycle than simply "recycled" paper products, with less of an environmental impact overall. Products made with PCW paper are usually labeled as such, and the more PCW content, the better.

**Pre-Consumer Waste**
Paper and paperboard waste collected during manufacturing or printing that never actually made it to the consumer. It includes scraps, trimmings, make-ready sheets, and unused copies which may have been over-ordered or over-printed. Products made with any amount of pre-consumer waste paper can be labeled as "recycled"; therefore be sure to look for products that include the highest amount of recycled content.

**Rightsize**
Rightsizing reduces packaging materials by designing to minimize empty space while still protecting the product inside. This design approach will help save natural resources in the manufacture of the packaging and the ensuing transport of the products.

**Sludge**
The waste material left over after pulping and deinking in the papermaking or recycling process. Although some sludge is produced in the virgin papermaking process, far more is produced in the deinking process before recycling. Other materials that drop into the sludge include clay coatings, fillers from the previous paper, paper clips and staples, fibers too short to be made into paper, leftover ink, and so on. To avoid sludge, minimizing ink coverage on a printed piece can help.

**Triple Bottom Line**
The pursuit of growth that is in balance with ecological, social, and economic needs.

**Upcycle**

A term coined by William McDonough and Michael Braungart, upcycle refers to the process of converting a material into something of similar or greater value in its second life.

**Virgin Tree Fiber**

Virgin tree paper is made using 100% brand new pulp. The methods used to harvest trees for paper production are endangering the survival of forests all over the world. Logging companies engage in clearcutting forests, which involves the felling and removal of all trees from a given tract of forest.

**Volatile Organic Compounds**

Carbon compounds that evaporate or vaporize readily under normal conditions. Indoors, they can cause eye, nose, and throat irritation; headaches; loss of coordination; nausea; liver and kidney damage; and issues with the central nervous system. Volatile organic compounds (VOCs) are also suspected to cause cancer in humans. VOCs, such as methane, contain greenhouse gases that contribute to increased global warming. In the graphic design profession, VOCs can be found most readily in printing inks, toners, plastics, and adhesives.

**Zero Waste**

Zero waste suggests that the entire concept of waste should be eliminated. It means considering the entire life cycle of products and services from the design phase with waste prevention in mind. Using recycled or compostable materials that are again recycled or composted after use are just two strategies that can help lead to a zero waste design project.

## ENDNOTES

1. Canopy's Second Harvest Campaign. Canopy.
2. Guides for the Use of Environmental Marketing Claims ("Green Guides"). 2012. Federal Register Notices Vol. 77, No. 197. 16 CFR Part 260. Federal Trade Commission.

# FURTHER READING

**Sustainable Design**

*The Upcycle: Beyond Sustainability—Designing for Abundance*
William McDonough and Michael Braungart
North Point Press, 2013

*Design Futuring*
Tony Fry
Bloomsbury Academic, 2008

*User Experience in the Age of Sustainability: A Practitioner's Blueprint*
Kem-Laurin Kramer
Morgan Kaufmann, 2012

*Design Is the Problem*
Nathan Shedroff
Rosenfeld Media, 2009

**Design Citizenship**

*The Design Activist's Handbook: How to Change the World (Or at Least Your Part of It) with Socially Conscious Design*
Noah Scalin and Michelle Taute
HOW Books, 2012

*Developing Citizen Designers*
Elizabeth Resnick
Bloomsbury Academic, 2016

**Systems Thinking**

*Biomimicry: Innovation Inspired by Nature*
Janine M. Benyus
Harper Perennial, 2002

*The Systems View of Life: A Unifying Vision*
Professor Fritjof Capra and Pier Luigi Luisi
Cambridge University Press, 2014

*Thinking in Systems: A Primer*
Donella H. Meadows
Chelsea Green Publishing, 2008

# INDEX